The Ultimate Vegetarian Cookbook

Susie Ward

CHARTWELL
BOOKS, INC.

A QUANTUM BOOK

This edition published in 2011 by
CHARTWELL BOOKS, INC.
A division of BOOK SALES, INC.
276 Fifth Avenue, Suite 206
New York, New York 10001
USA

ISBN-13: 978-0-7858-2848-8

QUMTUVC

This book is produced by
Quantum Publishing
6 Blundell Street

London N7 9BH

Digitized by Quadrum Solutions, Mumbai, Indian

www.quadrumltd.com

Cover design by Dave Jones, www.euro-designs.info

Consultant Editors: Susie Ward and Caroline Smith

Managing Editor: Julie Brooke

Project Editor: Samantha Warrington

Assistant Editor: Jo Morley

Production Manager: Rohana Yusof

Publisher: Sarah Bloxham

Printed in Singapore by

Star Standard Industries Pte Ltd

The material in this publication previously appeared in *Complete Vegetarian Cookbook, The Almost Vegetarian Cookbook, The Bread Book, Chinese Vegetarian Cooking, Cooking with Yoghurt, Indian Vegetarian Cooking, Meal Planner / Healthy Cooking, Microwave Cooking for Vegetarians, Microwave Library / Cooking with Vegetables, The Pasta and Pizza Cookbook, Sensational Salads, Tapas, The Wholefood Cookbook.*

Contents

Introduction

Vegetarian food is different, delicious, nourishing and fresh. It can turn cooking, as well as eating, into a daily pleasure. The simple goodness of fresh ingredients in a loaf of homemade bread and a bowl of soup often gives more satisfaction than the most complicated concoction smothered in a butter-rich sauce. Learning to cook without meat and fish is something of a challenge, as we are so used to having one or the other as the main ingredient of the meal. However, the effort is worthwhile—as your tastebuds will tell you.

Vegetarianism and wholefood cooking are enjoying a new surge of popularity in the developed world as a reaction to the high-fat, high-sugar, high-starch junk foods that have so dominated our diets for the past 30 years.

The first pleasure of wholefood cooking is the goodness it brings to your table. The freshness and flavor of natural foods, unrefined and free from additives, offer a range of ingredients that are infinitely rich and subtle. But wholefood eating doesn't only satisfy the palate, it brings long-term health benefits too.

Our Western diet tends to be soft, sweet and high in animal fats. Over-refined and processed foods contain fewer vitamins and minerals, and chemical additives can cause unpleasant side effects. The foods closest to nature—fresh fruit and vegetables, unrefined grains, nuts and pulses—are high in vitamins and minerals, high in fiber and low in fat. They provide cheaper protein and satisfy at moderate calorie levels.

So vegetarianism also makes economic and ecological sense. A field of soy beans will yield 30 times as much protein as the same field used to rear beef cattle. Surprisingly though, it is still the case that agricultural land is devoted to feeding animals, far more than to growing crops. A further cruel reality is that economic pressures tend to encourage under-developed countries to export their grain as cattle feed for richer countries.

For many people, it is the slaughter of animals for food which has made them turn to a vegetarian life, as has the practice of keeping factory farmed hens in tiny cages for the duration of their short lives. In addition, though modern food production methods have effectively made meat much cheaper than ever before, inevitably the taste of mass-produced meat, from animals reared on chemically treated feed and injected with hormones, suffers from a uniform blandness. Considerations such as this have given many a less ideological but as valid a reason to prefer a largely wholefood and vegetarian lifestyle.

Other healthy products, for instance yogurt, complement much vegetarian fare. It is perhaps the best known of all cultured milk products and has had an amazing rise from relative obscurity as an indigenous Middle Eastern food to world-wide popularity—all within the last 30 or so years. It has been credited with extraordinary properties, particularly since scientists, about 100 years ago, became fascinated by the microbiological processes that take place in milk during fermentation. At that time a Russian scientist, Ilya Mechnikov, isolated the bacteria found in yogurt. It is recorded that ancient physicians used to prescribe sour milk for dysentery, tuberculosis, liver problems and various other illnesses. It was found that acidic milk is more easily digested than ordinary milk, and modern medical practitioners have used it to counteract the effect of some antibiotics, that destroy beneficial intestinal flora. Today aficionados of yogurt are able to enjoy a wide selection of products and the truly devoted sleuth may be able to track down some very unusual varieties.

So you see, you don't have to be a vegetarian to enjoy this book, but you might adopt a new attitude to eating. For instance, you could break away from the traditional three-course meal and serve several complementary dishes at once, as in Eastern countries, or you could serve one large salad as a main course and offer homemade bread and an assortment of dressings. The best thing about vegetarianism is that it is an adventure and opens up new possibilities to the diner, and to the cook.

SOUPS

The goodness of soup has always appealed to those who appreciate real home cooking. Hearty and wholesome, soups preserve all the vitamins and nutrients of their cooked ingredients, but contain relatively few calories. And in France country folk say that you can always tell a true cook by her soup!

Bean Soup

Serves 4–6

250 g (9 oz) fava beans
1–2 tbsp oil
1 onion, chopped
1 clove garlic, chopped
2 carrots, chopped
2 stalks celery, sliced
200 g (7 oz) tomatoes, peeled (or a small can)
1 slice lemon
light soy sauce
salt and freshly ground black pepper
parsley

1   Soak the beans overnight. Bring to a boil in a large saucepan of water about 1.2 l (2½ pt) and simmer until tender.
2   Meanwhile, heat oil in a frying pan and cook onion and garlic until soft. Stir in carrots, celery and tomatoes, in that order.
3   Add vegetables to the saucepan with the cooked beans. Add the slice of lemon and soy sauce. Taste and adjust seasoning. Heat through and serve sprinkled with chopped parsley. The soup may be partly blended if you like.

Beet and Cabbage Borscht

Serves 6–8

butter or margarine
450 g (1 lb) cooked beets, peeled and diced
2 tbsp flour
2 tbsp vinegar
700 g (1½ lb) red cabbage, finely grated
1 bay leaf
1 clove garlic, crushed
1 tbsp sugar
2 l (4 pt) vegetable stock
salt and freshly ground black pepper
150 ml (5 fl oz) sour cream

1   Heat the butter add the beets and toss for 1 minute. Add the flour and stir well off the heat. Return to the heat and add the vinegar, mixing it in well.
2   Add the cabbage, bay leaf, garlic, sugar, stock, salt and pepper. Bring to a boil and then simmer, covered, for 1 hour, adding a little more stock if necessary. Serve hot with a generous spoonful of sour cream in each bowl.

Harvest Soup

Serves 4–6

1–2 tsp oil
1 onion, chopped
350 g (12 oz) pumpkin, peeled and diced
250 g (9 oz) carrots, sliced
2 potatoes
juice of half a lemon
1.1 l (2½ pt) stock
salt and freshly ground black pepper
1 zucchini, sliced
50 g (2 oz) green beans, sliced
basil leaves to garnish

1 Heat oil in a large saucepan and fry onion until translucent.
2 Add pumpkin, carrots and potatoes and pour over lemon juice. Sweat, covered, for 5 minutes.
3 Add stock and seasoning and simmer until potatoes are cooked. Blend or partially blend the soup.
4 Add zucchini and beans and simmer for 4 more minutes. Check seasoning.
5 Serve garnished with basil leaves. This soup can also be served sprinkled with Parmesan cheese.

Cream of Cauliflower Soup

Serves 4

1 small cauliflower
salt and freshly ground black pepper
4 tbsp butter
25 g (1 oz) all-purpose flour
6 tbsp half and half
1–2 egg yolks
1 tbsp chopped chives
Toast to serve

1 Trim the outer leaves off the cauliflower and steam it whole in boiling salted water in a saucepan with the lid on until tender. Let the cauliflower cool and reserve the water.

2 Melt the butter in a saucepan and stir in the flour. Gradually stir in the cauliflower water, made up to 900 ml (2 pt) with fresh water.

3 Reserve some of the cauliflower florets for garnishing. Discard the tougher stalks and purée the rest in a blender. Add to the saucepan.

4 Beat the cream and egg yolks together in a bowl. Beat in some of the soup, then return to the saucepan. Add the reserved cauliflower florets. Heat through but do not boil. Season and add chopped chives. Serve with triangles of hot toast.

Lima Bean and Mushroom Chowder

Serves 4–6

100 g (4 oz) lima beans soaked overnight in cold water
1 tsp olive oil
2 onions, chopped
2 stalks celery, sliced
225 g (8 oz) potatoes, peeled and diced
100 g (4 oz) button mushrooms, sliced
50 g (2 oz) corn kernels
300 ml (½ pt) skim milk
salt
freshly ground black pepper
2 tbsp chopped parsley

1 Drain the beans and place in a large saucepan covered with fresh water. Boil vigorously for 10 minutes, then simmer for 35–40 more minutes, or until soft. Drain the beans and reserve 450 ml (15 fl oz) of the stock.

2 Heat the oil in a large saucepan and gently fry the onion. Add the celery and potato and cook for 2–3 minutes, stirring from time to time. Add the reserved stock and mushrooms, bring to a boil, cover and simmer for 10 minutes.

3 Add the beans, corn and milk, bring to a boil and simmer for 2–3 minutes. Season to taste.

4 Serve sprinkled with parsley. Serve slices of whole wheat bread separately.

Cheese and Onion Soup

Serves 4–6
1–2 tbsp oil
2 medium onions, sliced
1.1 l (2½ pt) stock
250 g (9 oz) potatoes
175 g (6 oz) grated Cheddar cheese
salt
light soy sauce

1 Heat oil in a large saucepan and stirfry onions until lightly browned. Add stock and bring to a boil.
2 Meanwhile, peel the potatoes and grate them into the saucepan. Turn down the heat and simmer until the potatoes have cooked and the soup has thickened.
3 Add the grated cheese, stirring to melt. Season to taste with salt and soy sauce. Serve with wholewheat bread and a crisp green salad.

Garlic Soup

Serves 4–6
1.1 l (2½ pt) vegetable stock
4 garlic cloves, crushed
3 tsp paprika
3 tsp cumin
salt and freshly ground black pepper
2 pieces bread, toasted
oil
6 eggs (optional)

1 Pour vegetable stock into a saucepan, add the garlic, paprika and cumin, and bring to a boil. Season.
2 Break the toast into cubes and put into hot soup bowls.
3 Place a saucepan on the heat, lightly oil, and fry the eggs until the white becomes firm. Put 1 egg into each soup bowl and pour the boiling soup over.

Curried Squash Soup

Serves 4

oil

1 large onion, chopped

2 tbsp curry powder

1 small squash about 700 g/1½ lb, peeled
and chopped

1 l (2 pt) vegetable stock

150 ml (5 fl oz) yogurt

2 tbsp mango chutney

1 Heat the oil, add the onion and cook until it has just softened but not browned. Stir in the curry powder and cook it for 1 minute. Add the squash and stir well.

2 Pour in the stock. Bring to a boil and then simmer until the squash is soft.

3 Blend the soup in a food processor or blender and return it to the saucepan.

4 Keep the soup warm while you mix the yogurt and chutney together. Stir into the soup and serve immediately.

Cook's Tip

If you prefer to make this in advance, don't add the yogurt mixture until you reheat it. You could serve with a little dried coconut and additional chutney if desired.

Tomato and Egg Flower Soup

Serves 6
250 g (9 oz) tomatoes, skinned
1 egg
2 scallions, finely chopped
1 tbsp oil
1 l (2 pt) water
2 tbsp light soy sauce
1 tsp cornstarch mixed with 2 tsp water

1 Skin the tomatoes by dipping them in boiling water for a minute or so and then peeling them. Cut into large slices. Beat the egg. Finely chop the spring onions.
2 Heat a wok or saucepan over a high heat. Add the oil and wait for it to smoke. Add the scallions to flavour the oil and then pour in the water.
3 Drop in the tomatoes and bring to a boil.
4 Stir in the soy sauce and very slowly pour in the beaten egg. Add the cornstarch and water mixture. Stir for a few minutes and serve.

Chinese Cabbage Soup

Serves 4–6
250 g (9 oz) Chinese cabbage
3–4 dried Chinese mushrooms, soaked in warm water for 30 minutes
2 tbsp oil
2 tsp salt
1 tbsp rice wine or dry sherry
900 ml (1½ pt) water
1 tsp sesame oil

1 Wash the cabbage and cut it into thin slices. Squeeze dry the soaked mushrooms. Discard the hard stalks and cut the mushrooms into small pieces. (Reserve the water in which the mushrooms have been soaked for use later.)
2 Heat a wok or large pot until hot, add the oil and wait for it to smoke. Add the cabbage and mushrooms and stir.
3 Add the salt, wine, water and the mushroom soaking water. Bring to a boil.
4 Stir in the sesame oil and serve.

Cantonese Hot and Sour Soup

Serves 6

3 dried Chinese mushrooms, soaked in warm
    water for 30 minutes
900 ml (1½ pt) water
2 cakes tofu
50 g (2 oz) Sichuan preserved vegetables
    (available from Asian shops)
50 g (2 oz) Chinese pickled vegetables, such
    as cucumber, cabbage or green beans
    (available from Asian shops, or make your own,
    see page 125)
2 slices fresh ginger, grated
2 scallions, finely chopped
1 tsp salt
2 tbsp rice wine or sherry
1 tbsp dark soy sauce
freshly ground black pepper to taste
1 tsp sesame oil
1 tsp cornstarch with 2 tsp water

1   Squeeze the mushrooms dry after soaking.
    Discard the hard stalks and cut mushrooms
    into thin shreds. Reserve the water.
2   Thinly shred the tofu, Sichuan preserved
    vegetables, pickled vegetables and ginger. Finely
    chop the scallions.
3   In a wok or large pot, bring the water to a boil and
    add the mushroom water. Add all the ingredients
    and seasonings and simmer for 2 minutes.
4   Add the sesame seed oil and thicken the soup
    by stirring in the cornstarch and water mixture.
    Serve hot!

Chinese Mushroom Soup

Serves 4
6 dried Chinese mushrooms, soaked in warm
  water for 30 minutes
600 ml (1 pt) water
2 tsp cornstarch
1 tbsp/15 ml (½ fl oz) cold water
3 egg whites
2 tsp salt
1 scallion, finely chopped

1 Squeeze dry the mushrooms after soaking. Discard the hard stalks and cut each mushroom into thin slices. Reserve the mushroom water.
2 Mix the cornstarch with the water to make a smooth paste. Comb the egg whites with your fingers to loosen them.
3 Mix the water and the mushroom water in a saucepan and bring to a boil. Add the mushrooms and cook for about 1 minute. Now add the cornstarch and water mixture, stir and add the salt.
4 Pour the egg whites very slowly into the soup, stirring constantly.
5 Garnish with the finely chopped scallions and serve hot.

Corn and Asparagus Soup

Serves 4
175 g (6 oz) white asparagus
1 egg white
1 tbsp cornstarch
2 tbsp water
600 ml (1 pt) water
1 tsp salt
100 g (4 oz) corn
1 scallion, finely chopped, to garnish

1 Cut the asparagus spears into small cubes.
2 Beat the egg white lightly. Mix the cornstarch with the water to make a smooth paste.
3 Bring the water to a rolling boil. Add the salt, corn and asparagus. When the water starts to boil again, add the cornstarch and water mixture, stirring constantly.
4 Add the egg white very slowly and stir. Serve hot, garnished with finely chopped scallions.

Cream of Nettle Soup

Serves 6
900 g (2 lb) young nettles
2 tbsp butter
1 small onion, chopped
25 g (1 oz) flour
900 ml (2 pts) milk
salt and freshly ground black pepper
2 egg yolks
1 tbsp half and half
cream and croutons to serve

1   Wearing gloves, pick the young nettle leaves
    before the plants flower. Discard the stalks, wash
    the leaves and press them into a saucepan with
    only the water that is clinging to them. Cover the
    saucepan and cook until soft (5–8 minutes). Purée
    in a blender.
2   Heat the butter in a saucepan and cook the onion
    until soft. Stir in the flour, then a little milk and cook
    until thick. Stir in enough of the remaining milk
    to make a very thin sauce. Add the milk and the
    sauce to the nettles. Season well.
3   Beat the egg yolks with the cream. Stir in a little
    of the soup, then return to the saucepan. Heat
    through and check seasoning.
4   To serve, add a swirl of cream and some croutons
    to each bowl.

Spinach Soup

Serves 4–6
oil
1 large onion, sliced
750 g (1½ lbs) spinach, washed and picked over
1 clove garlic, crushed
3 sprigs of thyme, leaves picked
1 l (2 pts) vegetable stock
300 ml (10 fl oz) yogurt
salt and freshly ground black pepper

1   Heat the oil, add the onion and cook until it has
    just softened but not browned. Add the spinach,
    garlic and thyme, and stir. Add the stock, bring to
    a boil and simmer, covered, for 15 minutes.
2   Purée the soup in a blender, adding the yogurt
    slowly. Adjust the seasoning. Serve hot or cold.

Cook's Tip
Use frozen spinach if you prefer; about 450 g (1 lb)
would do.

Mushroom Soup

Serves 6
butter or oil
1 large onion, sliced
350 g (12 oz) mushrooms, sliced
grated nutmeg
1 tbsp flour
450 ml (15 fl oz) vegetable stock
300 ml (10 fl oz) yogurt
2 tbsp sherry (optional)

1 Heat the butter or oil and cook the onion until it has just softened but not browned. Add the mushrooms, stir and leave them to cook for 2 minutes. Add more butter if necessary.
2 Add the nutmeg and flour and stir well. Slowly add the stock, stirring until the mixture is smooth.
3 Bring the soup to a boil then simmer for 5 minutes. Stir in the yogurt and just warm it through. Add the sherry (optional). Garnish with fresh mushrooms and serve hot with cheese toast.

Carrot and Cilantro Soup

Serves 6–8
oil or butter
1 medium onion, sliced
700 g (1½ lb) carrots, sliced
1 tsp ground cilantro
900 ml (2 pt) vegetable stock
150 ml (5 fl oz) sour cream
salt and freshly ground black pepper
parsley to garnish

1 Heat the oil, add the onion and cook until it has just softened but not browned. Add the carrots and cilantro and stir well. Leave the carrots to cook gently for 3 minutes.
2 Pour in the stock and bring the mixture to a boil, then simmer, covered, for 25 minutes.
3 Purée the soup in a blender, adding the sour cream. Adjust the seasoning. Serve very cold, garnished with parsley.

Pumpkin Soup

Serves 4–6
1 tbsp sunflower oil
1 onion, chopped
350 g (12 oz) pumpkin or squash, peeled, and diced (pulp removed)
225 g (8 oz) carrots, diced
2 potatoes, diced
600 ml (1 pt) vegetable stock
2 small zucchini, thinly sliced
freshly ground black pepper
chopped parsley
rosemary to garnish

1 Place the oil and onion in a saucepan and cook for 2–3 minutes, to soften.
2 Add the pumpkin or squash, carrots, potatoes and stock. Bring to a boil, cover and simmer for 15 minutes, or until the vegetables are nearly tender.
3 Add the zucchini and cook for 5 minutes more.
4 Purée half the soup, blend with the remaining soup and season with pepper, to taste.
5 Reheat if necessary and serve in single bowls. Make sure some of the zucchini floats on the top to decorate.
6 Sprinkle with parsley to serve. The golden color of this soup, and its ingredients, make it a good choice to serve in the Fall. Add rosemary to garnish.

Watercress and Potato Soup

Serves 4–6
butter or margarine
1 medium onion, chopped
450 g (1 lb) peeled and sliced potatoes
2 bunches watercress
salt and freshly ground black pepper
600 ml (1 pt) vegetable stock
450 ml (15 fl oz) yogurt
1 egg

1 Heat the butter, add the onion and cook until it has just softened but not browned.
2 Add the potatoes and watercress and stir. Season with salt and peeper and leave on low heat for 3 minutes. Pour in the stock and simmer for 20 minutes.
3 Mix the yogurt with the egg. When the potatoes are soft, purée the soup in a blender, adding the yogurt mixture slowly, as the machine is running. If you wish to serve warm, return to the saucepan, and stir over low heat to avoid curdling.
4 If you prefer the soup cold, chill for about 1 hour, then serve.

Watercress Soup

Serves 4
butter
1 large onion, chopped
225 g (8 oz) potatoes, peeled
1.1 l (2½ pt) stock
salt and freshly ground black pepper
3 bunches watercress
half and half

1 Melt the butter in a large saucepan, add the onion and cook, stirring, until transparent.
2 Add the potatoes, stock and seasoning and bring to a boil, then simmer until potatoes can be mashed with a fork.
3 Wash the watercress and discard tough stalks and yellow leaves. Reserve a few sprigs for garnish, roughly chop the rest and add to the soup. Continue cooking for 2 minutes.
4 Allow the soup to cool slightly, then purée in a blender. Leave to cool completely. Taste and adjust seasoning. Chill and serve with sprigs of watercress to garnish and a swirl of cream.

Gazpacho

Serves 4–6
450 g (1 lb) large ripe tomatoes
1 large onion
2 cloves garlic
1 green pepper
1 red pepper
½ cucumber
2 slices wholewheat bread
3 tbsp olive oil
3 tbsp wine vinegar
300 ml (10 fl oz) tomato juice
300 ml (10 fl oz) water
salt and freshly ground black pepper

1 Skin tomatoes, discard seeds and juice and chop the flesh. Peel and finely chop the onion and garlic. Remove pith and seeds from peppers and dice. Peel and dice the cucumber. Cut the crusts from the bread and dice.

2 Put vegetables and bread in a large bowl, pour over the remaining ingredients, stir and season. Chill well—overnight is best for a good tasty soup.

3 You can partly blend the soup if you wish, or blend all of it, in which case offer small bowls of chopped onions, tomatoes, peppers, cucumber and croutons to garnish.

Persian Cucumber Soup

Serves 6

1 large cucumber, finely grated
600 ml (1 pt) yogurt
2 tbsp tarragon vinegar
dill
2 tbsp raisins soaked in 2 tbsp brandy for a
   few hours
2 hard-boiled eggs, finely chopped
1 large clove garlic, crushed
1 tsp sugar
150 ml (5 fl oz) cream
salt and freshly ground black pepper

1 Combine all the ingredients and stir thoroughly. Refrigerate for a minimum of 3 hours and serve very cold.

Variation

You may prefer mint or tarragon to dill, and chopped apples, celery, fennel and radishes can also be used instead of cucumber.

Avocado Soup

Serves 4

2 large ripe avocados
600 ml (1 pt) yogurt
1 clove garlic, crushed
juice of 1 lemon
salt and freshly ground black pepper

1 Halve the avocados, remove the stones and peel them.
2 Blend all the ingredients together. Serve very chilled, garnished with chives if desired.

Cook's Tip

The thickness of the soup will depend on the size of the avocados and the thickness of the yogurt. Thin it down with a little milk or cream if you need to.

Cold Tomato Soup

Serves 6–8

600 ml (1 pt) tomato juice
600 ml (1 pt) yogurt
3 scallions, chopped
1 green pepper, chopped
1 large tomato, skinned and chopped
salt and freshly ground black pepper
ice cubes

1 Blend the juice and yogurt and pour the mixture into a large bowl. Add the onions, pepper and tomato and season to taste. Serve very chilled, with some ice cubes floating in the soup.

Variation

You can add or subtract ingredients to this recipe: Try sliced avocados; fresh basil; chopped olives; finely-diced cucumber; raw mushrooms; chopped fennel; or croutons.

Red-hot Lentil Soup

Serves 6
3 tbsp butter
1 large onion, chopped
1 clove garlic, chopped
1 slice fresh ginger, unpeeled
1 slice lemon
225 g (8 oz) red lentils
1.5 l (3 pt) water
salt
pinch of paprika
1 green chili, deseeded and chopped

1 Heat 2 tbsp butter in a saucepan and add the onion, garlic, ginger and lemon. Sweat with the lid on over low heat for 5 minutes.
2 Add the lentils and the water (small red lentils do not need to be pre-soaked) and season with salt and paprika. Cook for about 40 minutes until the lentils have thickened the soup.
3 Heat the remaining butter in a saucepan and quickly fry the chili. Serve the soup with a chili topping.

Broccoli and Orange Soup

Serves 6
1 medium onion, chopped
1 tbsp oil
450 g (1 lb) broccoli, chopped
juice of 2 oranges
600 ml (1 pt) vegetable stock
300 ml (½ pt) yogurt
1 tbsp cornstarch
2 tbsp water
salt and freshly ground black pepper

1 Heat the oil and cook the onion until it has just softened but not browned.
2 Add the broccoli, reserve some small pieces for garnish, and stir. Cook, covered, for a few minutes and then add the orange juice and stock. Bring to a boil, cover and simmer for about 20 minutes, until the broccoli is soft. Purée the soup in a blender.
3 Mix the cornstarch and water into a smooth paste and stir into the soup with salt and pepper to taste. Return the soup to the heat and cook for five more minutes.
4 Serve, garnished with the reserved broccoli and the orange zest.

Cook's Tip
Use frozen broccoli if fresh is not available. Serve cold if preferred.

HORS D'OEUVRES AND APPETIZERS

International cuisine offers a wide selection of vegetarian and wholefood appetizers and first courses. Vegetable pastes and pâtés take a variety of forms, from Greek hummus and Egyptian fava bean pâté to Mexican guacamole and Italian-inspired zucchini molds. Stuffed vegetables—such as eggplants and artichokes—and deep-fried mouthfuls, including Indian samosas, Chinese spring rolls and Bulgarian eggs, tempt from the four corners of the world.

Israeli Avocado Cream

Serves 4
1 large avocado
75 g (3 oz) cream cheese
½ small onion, finely chopped
dash Tabasco
2 tbsp lemon juice
salt and freshly ground black pepper

1　Mash the flesh of the avocado. Add the remaining ingredients, mixing them in very well. Spoon the mixture into a serving dish and cover it well. Refrigerate until required. Do not make this too long before you intend to serve it, as avocado discolors quickly.

Cook's Tip
Serve with crudités or crackers as a dip or spread.

Guacamole

Serves 2–4
2 large ripe avocados
2 large ripe tomatoes
1 bunch scallions
1–2 tbsp olive oil
1–2 tbsp lemon juice
salt and freshly ground black pepper
2 green chilies

1　Remove the flesh from the avocados and mash. Skin the tomatoes, remove the seeds and chop finely. Chop the scallions.
2　Mix the vegetables together with olive oil and lemon juice and season to taste. Garnish with chopped green chilies and serve, chilled, as a dip or with hot pita bread (see page 141).

Yogurt and Tahini Dip

Serves 4–6
2 cloves garlic, crushed
150 ml (5 fl oz) tahini
150 ml (5 fl oz) yogurt
juice of 2 lemons
salt and freshly ground black pepper
chopped parsley

1 Blend everything together except the parsley until smooth. Taste and add more lemon juice and seasoning if necessary. Serve in a bowl and garnish with the chopped parsley.

Cook's Tip
Serve as a dip, with pita bread or crackers, or as an accompaniment to vegetables, salads or meat or fish dishes.

Celery Mousse

Serves 4–6
1 tbsp/15 ml (½ fl oz) agar agar
2 tbsp/30 ml (1 fl oz) boiling water
1 medium head of celery with leaves,
    roughly chopped
200 ml (7 fl oz) yogurt
squeeze lemon juice
1 small onion
parsley
150 g (5 oz) cottage cheese
salt and freshly ground black pepper

1 Dissolve the agar agar in the boiling water. Blend all the remaining ingredients, except the cottage cheese, feeding them into a blender or food processor slowly.
2 Add the dissolved agar agar and cottage cheese and blend it into the mixture. Pour into a moistened mold (a small ring mold looks nice). Refrigerate until set. Unmold and serve cold.

Hummus

Serves 4
225 g (8 oz) dried chickpeas, soaked overnight
1 bouquet garni
1 small onion, sliced
2 cloves garlic, crushed
juice of 2 lemons
4 tbsp tahini
3 tbsp olive oil
salt and freshly ground black pepper
1 tomato

1 Drain the chickpeas and place in a large saucepan with plenty of fresh water, the bouquet garni and onion. Bring to a boil then simmer gently for 1¾–2 hours, or until tender.
2 Drain, reserving a little of the cooking liquid. Discard the onion and bouquet garni.
3 Place the garlic, lemon juice, tahini, olive oil and seasoning in a food processor or blender. Add the cooked chickpeas and process to a smooth paste.
4 Add a little of the reserved cooking liquid if the paste is too thick, and stir rapidly.
5 Arrange the hummus in a dish and edge with halved tomato slices. Serve with warm pita bread.

Marinated Mushrooms

Serves 4
200 g (7 oz) button mushrooms
125 ml (4 fl oz) dry sherry
60 ml (4 tbsp) wine vinegar
60 ml (4 tbsp) vegetable stock
2 garlic cloves, crushed
1 onion, cut into eighths
1 tsp mustard
tbsp soy sauce
2 tbsp tomato purée
1 bay leaf

1 Place the mushrooms in a pan with all the other ingredients.
2 Heat gently for 10 minutes.
3 Allow to cool, remove bay leaf and transfer to a serving dish.
4 Cover and chill until required.

Blue Cheese Pâté

Serves 4
300 ml (2 fl oz) yogurt
100 g (4 oz) crumbled blue cheese
2–4 tbsp half and half

1 Drain the yogurt for about 5 hours. Remove the resulting cheese from the cloth carefully.
2 Blend the drained yogurt with the blue cheese and just enough cream to reach the required consistency. Refrigerate the mixture until needed. It will firm up considerably.

Cook's Tip
This mixture is useful as a filling for fruit (especially good with pears) or choux pastry, for stuffed tomatoes or celery, or as a salad dressing.

Tabbouleh with Tofu, Raisins and Pinenuts

An aromatic Middle Eastern salad made with bulgur wheat and fragrant fresh parsley and mint. Make ahead of time and leave for several hours or overnight before serving, to allow the flavors to develop.

Serves 4
125 g/4 oz bulgur wheat
7 tbsp extra-virgin olive oil
50 g/2 oz pine nuts
grated rind and juice of 1 lemon
2 garlic cloves, peeled and crushed
1 small cucumber
2 tomatoes
4 tbsp raisins
8 scallions, finely chopped
4 tbsp chopped fresh flat-leaf parsley
2 tbsp chopped fresh mint
250 g/9 oz firm tofu, cubed
salt and freshly ground black pepper

1 Put the bulgur wheat in a large bowl, cover with cold water, and leave to soak for at least 30 minutes. Heat 1 tablespoon of the olive oil in a small frying pan and stirfry the pine nuts briefly until golden. Drain on a plate lined with paper towels.

2 Mix the remaining olive oil with the lemon juice and garlic. Dice the cucumber and chop the tomatoes into small pieces.

3 Drain the bulgur wheat in a strainer, shaking out as much excess water as possible. Place in a bowl and add the cucumber, tomatoes, raisins, scallions, parsley, mint and tofu.

4 Pour the oil and lemon dressing over the mixture, and toss well. Add seasoning to taste. Cover the bowl and leave in a cool place for several hours or overnight. Sprinkle with the pine nuts and grated lemon rind when ready to serve.

Fava Bean Pâté

Serves 4
350 g (12 oz) fava beans, shelled
about 175 g (6 oz) cream cheese
salt and freshly ground black pepper
mint sprigs

1 If the beans are old, remove the skins before or after cooking. Boil lightly in salted water until tender.

2 Mash or put through a vegetable mill with enough cream cheese to make a thick paste. Season with salt and pepper. Press into single dishes and garnish each with a sprig of mint. Serve with triangles of wholewheat toast.

Stuffed Tomatoes

Serves 4

8 small tomatoes, or 3 beef (large) tomatoes

4 hard-boiled eggs, cooled and peeled

6 tbsp mayonnaise

1 tsp garlic paste

salt and freshly ground black pepper

1 tbsp parsley, chopped

1 tbsp white breadcrumbs if using beef (large) tomatoes

1 To skin the tomatoes, place in a saucepan of boiling water for 10 seconds, remove and plunge into a bowl of very cold water to stop the tomatoes from cooking further and going mushy. Peel off the skins using a sharp knife.

2 Slice the tops off the tomatoes and just enough from their bases so the tomatoes will sit squarely on the plate. Keep the tops only if using small tomatoes.

3 Remove the seeds and insides, either with a teaspoon or a small, sharp knife. Mash the eggs with the mayonnaise, garlic paste, salt, pepper and parsley.

4 Fill the tomatoes, firmly pressing the filling down. If using small tomatoes, replace the lids. If keeping to serve later, brush them with olive oil and sprinkle with black pepper to prevent them drying out. Cover with plastic film and keep.

Stuffed Peppers

Serves 4

2 large green peppers (or 1 red and 1 green)
225 g (8 oz) ricotta cheese
1 small pickled cucumber, finely chopped
1 tbsp chopped parsley
1 tbsp chopped dill (fresh or dried)
salt and freshly ground black pepper
crisp lettuce, to serve

1 Remove the stalk end of the peppers and discard the seeds. Mix the ricotta with the pickled cucumber, parsley, dill and salt and pepper.

2 Stuff the mixture into the peppers and refrigerate for several hours.

3 With a very sharp knife, cut the peppers into slices about 1 cm (½ in) thick. Serve the pepper slices on a bed of crisp lettuce.

Cook's Tip

Replace the ricotta with cheese curd or cottage cheese, or a mixture of low-fat soft cheeses.

Zucchini Molds

Serves 4

450 g (1 lb) zucchinis, sliced
1 onion, chopped
2 tbsp lemon juice
2 tsp fresh cilantro leaves, chopped
100 g (4 oz) cream cheese
salt and freshly ground black pepper
1 sachet agar agar
150 ml (¼ pt) plain low-fat yogurt
5 tbsp skim milk
1 egg yolk
1 tsp curry paste
chervil, chopped, to garnish

1   Place the zucchini and onions in a saucepan with 2 tbsp water and the lemon juice. Cover and cook over a gentle heat for 8–10 minutes, or until softened.

2   Cool slightly and purée in a food processor or blender. Add the cilantro leaves, cream cheese and seasoning and purée until smooth. Leave until lukewarm.

3   Sprinkle the agar agar over 2 tbsp water in a cup. Stand in a saucepan of hot water and stir to dissolve. Add to the purée and pour into four 150 ml (5 fl oz) ramekins. Chill for 1–1½ hours until set.

4   Meanwhile mix the yogurt, milk, egg yolk and curry paste together and heat gently until slightly thickened. Do not boil. Leave to cool.

5   Pour the sauce across the base of a serving dish, loosen the molds and turn out onto the dish. Garnish the tops of the molds with parlsey and serve.

Mozzarella and Avocado Bees

Serves 2

1 ripe avocado
100 g (4 oz) mozzarella cheese
1 tbsp olive oil
1 tbsp tarragon vinegar
salt and freshly ground black pepper

1   Cut the avocado in half and remove the stone. With a palette knife carefully remove the skin from each half of the avocado. Lay the avocado halves flat-side down and cut horizontally into 1 cm (¼ in) slices.

2   Cut semicircular slices from the mozzarella, with four extra semicircles for wings.

3   Arrange the cheese slices between the avocado slices to form the striped body of a bee, and arrange the wings at the sides.

4   Mix the oil and vinegar together and season well. Pour over the bees and serve.

Summer Posy Mousse

Serves 4–6

12 g (½ oz) (2 sachets) agar agar
2 tbsp warm water
2 eggs, separated, plus 1 egg white
150 ml (¼ pt) whipping cream
3 tbsp sour cream
100 g (4 oz) Roquefort cheese, crumbled
salt and freshly ground white pepper
few drops Tabasco

1   Put the agar agar and water into a small bowl and stand it in a saucepan of simmering water. Stir well until the agar agar has dissolved.
2   Beat the egg yolks with half of the cream, the sour cream and the agar agar. Mash in the cheese. Whip the remaining cream, fold into the mixture, season and add Tabasco sauce. Chill.
3   Whip the egg whites until soft peaks form. Fold them into the mixture. Oil a ring mold, pour in the mousse and chill until set.
4   Dip the mold into hot water, invert a plate over it and turn the mousse out. Fill the center with a posy of edible flowers and delicate leafy herbs. This dish can form the centerpiece of a summer lunch in the garden. Serve with brown bread.

Melon and Tangelo with Lemon Sauce

Serves 4

2 cantaloupes
2 tangelos, pith removed and segmented
2 tsp light brown sugar
juice 2 lemons
grated rind ½ lemon
twists lemon peel

1   Halve the melons, remove the seeds and scoop out balls of flesh using a vegetable baller.
2   Cut the tangelo segments in half, if large, and mix with the melon balls.
3   Scoop out the remaining melon flesh from the skins and place in a food processor or blender. Add the sugar, lemon juice and rind and blend.
4   Pour over the fruit and chill until required. To serve, divide the fruit between four tall glass dishes. Decorate the glass sides with twists of lemon peel.

Tomato and Mozzarella Salad

Serves 4

2 to 3 large tomatoes, thinly sliced	2 tbsp fresh basil
100 g (4 oz) fresh mozzarella cheese, thinly sliced	6 tbsp extra virgin olive oil
	salt and freshly ground black pepper

1 Arrange the tomatoes and mozzarella in alternating layers in a serving dish.
2 Garnish the salad with the basil.
3 Sprinkle the salad with the olive oil and salt and pepper. Serve.

Date and Cream Cheese Spread

Serves 4 (Makes 250 ml (8 fl oz))
50 g (2 oz) cream cheese
2 tbsp milk
225 g (8 oz) finely chopped fresh dates
1 tbsp finely grated lemon rind

1 Mix the cream cheese with the milk into a smooth consistency. Add the dates and lemon rind and mix together well.

Variation

Another delicious way to use fresh dates is to make a stuffing of cream cheese, chopped raisins, ginger or nuts to fill the dates, which are left whole but with the stone removed.

Cook's Tip

Fresh dates are so different from the more widely known semi-dried variety. This spread can be used on bread (try wholemeal) or as a cocktail appetizer on small crackers.

Crudités with Chili Tomato Dip

Serves 6–8

Your selection from the following, cut into manageable pieces,
carrots
celery
green, red and yellow peppers
cucumber
cauliflower florets
radishes
mushrooms

Chili Tomato Dip

300 ml (10 fl oz) low-fat plain yogurt
1 tbsp tomato paste
4 tbsp low fat mayonnaise
1 green chili, chopped
1 tbsp fresh chopped parsley

1 Prepare the vegetables and arrange them on a serving platter. Keep cold.

For the Chili Tomato Dip

1 Mix together the dip ingredients and place in a serving bowl.

Stuffed Garlic Mushrooms

Serves 4

16 portabella mushrooms, about 3 cm (1½ in) across
2 slices wholewheat bread, crumbled
150 ml (5 fl oz) warm milk
4 cloves garlic
50 g (2 oz) fresh mixed herbs, chopped
oil
salt and freshly ground black pepper

1 Preheat the oven to 180°C/350°F/Gas Mark 4.
2 Wipe the mushroom caps clean. Remove, chop and reserve stalks. Soak the breadcrumbs in milk until soft, then squeeze out excess milk.
3 In a mortar, pound the garlic with herbs and enough oil to make a paste. Pound in the stalks. Mix together with the breadcrumbs and season well with salt and pepper.
4 Spoon the filling into the mushroom caps and arrange them in a lightly oiled ovenproof dish. Bake for about 15 minutes until mushrooms are soft and juicy and filling has crisped a little on the top. Serve hot .

Garlic Mushrooms

Serves 4–6
6 tbsp butter
750 g (1½ lb) mushrooms, button or cap
few drops lemon juice
salt and freshly ground black pepper
2 cloves garlic, crushed
1 tbsp chopped cilantro or parsley

1 Heat the butter in a large saucepan. Add the mushrooms and sweat gently, covered, for 5 minutes, shaking occasionally.
2 Add the lemon juice, salt and pepper. Increase the heat, tossing the mushrooms well. Add the garlic, toss and cook for 2 minutes.
3 Add the cilantro or parsley and cook for 1 minute. Remove from the heat and serve.

Crispy "Seaweed"

Serves 4
750 g (1¾ lb) collard greens
600 ml (1 pt) oil for deep frying
1 tsp salt
1 tsp sugar

1 Wash and dry the spring green leaves and shred them with a sharp knife into the thinnest possible shavings. Spread them out on paper towels or put in a large colander to dry thoroughly.
2 Heat the oil in a wok or deep fryer. Before the oil gets too hot, turn off the heat for 30 seconds. Add the spring green shavings in several batches and turn the heat up to medium high. Stir with a pair of cooking chopsticks.
3 When the shavings start to float to the surface, scoop them out gently with a slotted spoon and drain on paper towels to remove as much of the oil as possible. Sprinkle the salt and sugar evenly on top and mix gently. Serve cold.

Variation
Dice half a red chili and add to the "seaweed" as a garnish, to give the dish a new dimension.

Sichuan-style Cucumber

Serves 4
1 cucumber
1 tsp salt
2 tbsp sugar
2 tbsp/30 ml (1 fl oz) vinegar
1 tbsp/15 ml (½ fl oz) chili oil

1 Split the cucumber in two lengthways and then cut each piece into strips like potato chips Sprinkle with the salt and leave for about 10 minutes to extract the bitter juices.
2 Remove each cucumber strip. Place it on a firm surface and soften it by gently tapping it with the blade of a cleaver or knife.
3 Place the cucumber strips on a plate. Sprinkle the sugar evenly over them and then add the vinegar and chili oil just before serving.

Vegetarian Spring Rolls

Serves 4

1 pack of 20 frozen spring roll skins
225 g (8 oz) fresh beansprouts
225 g (8 oz) young tender leeks or scallions
100 g (4 oz) carrots
100 g (4 oz) white mushrooms
flour and water paste (enough to brush the
    spring roll skins)
oil for deep frying
1½ tsp salt
1 tsp sugar
1 tbsp light soy sauce

Cook's Tip

Spring rolls are ideal for a buffet-style meal or as cocktail snacks. They can also be prepared in advance and frozen for up to 3 months.

1 Take the spring-roll skins out of the packet and leave them to defrost thoroughly under a damp cloth.

2 Wash and rinse the beansprouts in a bowl of cold water and discard the husks and other pieces that float to the surface. Drain.

3 Cut the leeks or scallions, carrots and mushrooms into thin shreds.

4 Heat 3–4 tbsp of oil in a preheated wok or large frying pan and stirfry all the vegetables for a few seconds. Add the salt, sugar and soy sauce and continue stirring for about 1–1½ minutes. Remove and leave to cool a little.

5 Cut each spring roll in half diagonally. Place about 2 tsp of the filling on the skin about a third of the way down, with the triangle pointing away from you. Lift the lower flap over the filling and roll once, then fold in both ends and roll once more.

6 Brush the upper edge with a little flour and water paste and roll into a neat package. Repeat until all the filling is used up.

7 Heat about 1.5 l (3 pt) oil in a wok or deep fryer until it smokes. Reduce the heat or even turn it off for a few minutes to cool the oil a little before adding the spring rolls. Deep fry 6–8 at a time for 3–4 minutes or until golden and crispy. Increase the heat to high again before frying each batch. As each batch is cooked, remove and drain it on paper towels. Serve hot with a dip such as soy sauce, vinegar, chili sauce or mustard.

Devilled Eggs

Serves 4
4 hard-boiled eggs, cut in half, lengthways
1½ tbsp onions, finely chopped
2 green chilies, finely chopped
1 tbsp cilantro leaves, chopped
½ tsp salt
2 tbsp potatoes, mashed
oil for deep frying
1 tbsp plain flour
60 ml (2 fl oz) water

1 Remove the egg yolks from the eggs and mix with the onions, chilies, cilantro leaves, salt and mashed potatoes. Put the mixture back into the egg whites. Chill for 30 minutes.

2 Heat the oil in a large saucepan over high heat. While the oil is heating up make a batter with the flour and water. Be careful not to let the oil catch fire.

3 Dip the eggs into the batter and slip into the hot oil. Fry until golden, turning once.

Stuffed Eggplants

Serves 4–8
4 eggplants
salt and freshly ground black pepper
olive oil
1 large onion, chopped
2–3 cloves garlic, crushed
4 large tomatoes, skinned and chopped
2 tbsp fresh herbs, chopped
100 g (4 oz) mozzarella cheese
4 tbsp brown breadcrumbs
a little butter

1 Preheat the oven to 200°C/400°F/Gas Mark 6. Wash the eggplants. Cut in half lengthways and score the cut surface deeply with a knife. Sprinkle with salt and leave, cut surface down, for 30 minutes.

2 Meanwhile heat 1–2 tbsp oil in a saucepan and fry the onion and garlic until translucent. Transfer to a bowl and mix in the tomatoes and chopped herbs.

3 Add more oil to the saucepan. Rinse the eggplants and pat dry. Place them cut surface down in the saucepan and cook gently for about 15 minutes. They absorb a lot of oil, so you will need to keep adding more.

4 Scoop some of the flesh out of the eggplants, mash it and mix with the rest of the filling. Season well. Pile the filling onto the eggplants and top with cubed pieces of mozzarella.

5 Sprinkle with breadcrumbs and dot with butter. Place eggplants in a greased ovenproof dish and bake for 20 minutes until the cheese has melted and the breadcrumbs are crispy.

Artichokes with Tomato Sauce

Serves 4
4 large artichokes
1–2 tbsp oil
1 large onion, chopped
2 cloves garlic, chopped
400 g (15 oz) canned tomatoes, mashed
1 tbsp tomato paste
2 tsp fresh oregano, chopped
salt and freshly ground black pepper
lemon juice

1 Rinse the artichokes thoroughly in cold water and leave them upside down to drain. Bring a very large saucepan of salted water to a boil, put the artichokes in and boil vigorously for 30–50 minutes, depending on the size. When an outer leaf comes away at a gentle tug, they are ready.

2 Meanwhile, make the sauce. Heat the oil in a saucepan and fry the onion and garlic until transparent. Add the tomatoes, tomato paste and oregano and reduce until the sauce is of pouring consistency but not sloppy. Season with salt and pepper and a dash of lemon juice to taste.

3 Drain the artichokes. When cool, pull out the tiny inner leaves and the hairy inedible choke. Spoon in some tomato sauce. Stand each artichoke in a pool of sauce on a single dish and serve.

Bulgarian Eggs

Serves 4
4 eggs
300 ml (10 fl oz) yogurt
1 small clove garlic, crushed
salt and freshly ground black pepper
½ tsp paprika
2 tbsp butter, melted

1 Softly poach the eggs. Mix the yogurt with the garlic, salt and pepper and warm it through gently but don't let it boil. Spoon it into four shallow dishes. Place one egg, well drained, into each dish. Add the paprika to the melted butter and drizzle it onto the eggs. Serve immediately, with hot French bread or pita bread.

Cook's Tip
This amount makes a good appetizer or very light supper dish. Double the quantity for a more substantial meal.

Pakoras

Serves 4 (Makes 450 g
   (1 lb) vegetables)
4 tbsp chickpea flour
2 tsp oil
1 tsp baking powder
½ tsp salt
6 tbsp water
oil for deep frying
Any of the following vegetables can be used:
   eggplants, cut into very thin rounds
   onions, cut into 0.25 cm (⅛ in) rings
   potatoes, cut into very thin rounds
   cauliflower, cut into 1.5 cm (¾ in) florets
   chili, left whole
   pumpkin, cut into thin slices
   green pepper, cut into thin strips

1 Mix the flour, 2 tsp oil, baking powder, salt and water together and beat until smooth. Wash the vegetable slices and pat dry.
2 Heat the oil in a large saucepan until very hot. Dip a slice of vegetable in the batter and put into the hot oil. Place as many slices as you can in the oil. Fry until crisp and golden. Drain and serve with mint or cilantro chutney.

Samosas

Serves 4–6
3 tbsp oil
¼ tsp cumin seeds
450 g (1 lb) potatoes, diced into 1.2 cm
   (½ in) cubes
1 green chili, finely chopped
pinch turmeric
½ tsp salt
75 g (3 oz) peas
1 tsp ground roasted cumin (oven-roasted
   for 5 minutes)

Dough
225 g (8 oz) all-purpose flour
1 tsp salt
3 tbsp oil
90 ml (3 fl oz) oil for deep frying

1 Heat the oil in a large saucepan over medium-high heat and add the cumin seeds. Let them sizzle for a few seconds.
2 Add the potatoes and green chili and fry for 2–3 minutes. Add the turmeric and salt and, stirring occasionally, cook for 5 minutes.
3 Add the peas and the ground roasted cumin. Stir to mix. Cover, lower heat and cook for 10 more minutes until the potatoes are tender. Cool.
4 Meanwhile, sift the flour and salt together. Rub in the oil. Add enough water to form a stiff dough. Knead for 10 minutes until smooth.
5 Divide into 12 balls. Roll each ball into a round of about 15 cm (6 in) across. Cut in half. Pick up one half, flatten it slightly and form a cone, sealing the overlapping edge with a little water. Fill the cone with 1½ tsp of the filling and seal the top with a little water. In a similar way, make all the samosas.
6 Heat oil in a large saucepan over medium heat. Put in as many samosas as you can into the hot oil and fry until crisp and golden. Drain. Serve with a chutney.

SALADS

Salads today have come a long way from the tossed green version. All kinds of vegetables and fruit—homely and exotic—have joined the cast list in the modern salad repertoire. The influence of Californian and Mediterranean cuisines vie with those of the East to make your choice as interesting as possible.

Swedish Tomato Salad

Serves 6

6 large tomatoes, seeded and halved
175 ml (6 fl oz) walnut oil
6 tbsp white wine vinegar
2 garlic cloves, crushed
¾ tsp dried dill
¼ tsp sugar
¼ tsp honey
½ tsp Dijon-style mustard
2 tbsp chopped fresh chives
½ tsp salt
¼ tsp freshly ground black pepper
6 to 8 lettuce leaves
6 fresh parsley sprigs

1 Put the tomatoes, cut-side down, in a shallow dish.
2 Put the walnut oil, vinegar, garlic, dill, sugar, honey, mustard, chives, salt and pepper in a jar with a tightly fitting lid. Cover tightly and shake vigorously until all the ingredients are blended.
3 Pour the dressing over the tomatoes. Chill the salad for 2½ hours. Every 30 minutes spoon the dressing over the tomatoes.
4 Line a serving dish with lettuce leaves. Remove the tomatoes from the dish and place them on the lettuce leaves. Pour the dressing over the tomatoes. Garnish with the parsley sprigs and serve.

Tomato Salad with Light Vinaigrette

Serves 4

3 beef (large) tomatoes
½ onion, finely sliced
few black olives
300 ml (½ pt) Light Vinaigrette (see page 118)

1 Slice the tomatoes horizontally. Arrange either in a large bowl with onion in between layers, or on a large plate. Sprinkle with black olives.
2 Pour over the dressing and serve.

Cook's Tip
If keeping to serve later, add the dressing 20 minutes before required.

Pine Nuts and Watercress

Serves 4

2 tbsp pine nuts
2 large bunches watercress
100 g (4 oz) fresh parsley, finely chopped
90 g (3½ oz) fresh chives, finely chopped
175 ml (6 fl oz) Lemon Dressing (see page 120)

1 Preheat the oven to 180°C/350°F/Gas Mark 4. Put the pine nuts on a baking tray and toast them in the oven until browned, about 8 to 10 minutes.
2 Put the watercress, parsley and chives in a salad bowl. Add the Lemon Dressing and toss. Add the pine nuts and toss again.

Italian Fontina Cheese Salad

Serves 6

2 large sweet yellow peppers, seeded and halved
2 large sweet red peppers, seeded and halved
225 g (8 oz) Fontina cheese, diced
50 g (2 oz) stoned green olives, thinly sliced
6 tbsp olive oil
1½ tsp Dijon-style mustard
3 tbsp half and half
1 tbsp chopped scallion
¾ tsp salt
1 tsp freshly ground black pepper
1 tbsp chopped fresh parsley

1 Preheat the broiler. Place the yellow and red peppers on a baking tray and broil until the skins are blistered and slightly blackened, about 10 to 15 minutes. Remove the peppers from the heat.
2 When the peppers are cool enough to handle, remove the blistered skin. Cut the peppers into strips about 9 mm (⅜ in) wide. Put the pepper strips, Fontina cheese and olives in a serving bowl.
3 Put the olive oil, mustard, cream, scallion, salt and pepper in a jar with a tightly fitting lid. Cover tightly and shake until well blended.
4 Pour the dressing over the salad and toss. Chill the salad for 1 to 2 hours. Garnish with the chopped parsley and toss again lightly before serving.

Japanese Cucumber Salad

Serves 4

2 medium-sized cucumbers, thinly sliced
1 tsp salt
4 tbsp rice wine vinegar
2 tbsp light soy sauce
1 tsp sugar
2 tsp white sesame seeds
nori (optional garnish)

1 Put the cucumber slices in a colander. Sprinkle with the salt. Let the cucumber slices drain for 30 minutes. Remove the cucumber slices from the colander. Put the slices between two layers of paper towels and pat them dry.
2 In a jar with a tightly fitting lid, put the vinegar, soy sauce and sugar. Cover tightly and shake well until the sugar dissolves.
3 Put the cucumber slices in a salad bowl. Add the dressing and toss lightly.
4 Toast the sesame seeds in a dry frying pan over high heat, shaking the pan frequently. When the seeds begin to jump, remove them from the pan and crush them with a pestle. Sprinkle the crushed sesame seeds on the salad, with the nori (optional) and serve.

Orange and Walnut Salad

Serves 4
3 plump heads endive
2 large sweet oranges, peel and pith
   removed, segmented
75 g (3 oz) walnuts, chopped

Mustard dressing
2 tbsp walnut oil
pinch mustard powder
1 tbsp orange juice
1 tbsp lemon juice

1 Mix the endive slices, oranges and half of the walnuts together and place in a serving dish.
2 Sprinkle over the remaining walnuts.
3 Whisk the walnut oil and mustard powder together, then gradually whisk in the orange and lemon juices.
4 Pour the dressing over the salad and serve immediately.

Mixed Greens and Mushrooms with Raspberry Vinaigrette

Serves 4
4 tbsp pine nuts
2 heads lettuce
2 heads endive
1 small head radicchio
225 g (8 oz) stemmed small mushrooms

Raspberry vinaigrette
4 tbsp olive oil
2 tbsp raspberry vinegar
1 finely chopped shallot
1 tsp Dijon mustard
2 tsp half and half
salt and freshly ground black pepper

1 Preheat the oven to 180°C/350°F/Gas Mark 4. Place the pine nuts in a shallow baking dish and toast them in the oven until lightly browned, about 5 minutes. Remove from oven and set aside.
2 Wash and gently dry the lettuce, endive and radicchio. Tear the lettuce and radicchio into bite-sized pieces. Cut the endive into thin slices. Put the greens into a large salad bowl. Add the mushrooms and toasted pine nuts.
3 In a mixing bowl combine the olive oil, vinegar, shallot, mustard, cream, salt and pepper. Whisk until the vinaigrette is smooth and well blended.
4 Pour the vinaigrette over the greens and toss well. Serve at once.

Orange and Mixed Green Salad

Serves 4

½ head lettuce

2 large navel oranges

225 g (8 oz) carrots, cut into strips

50 g (2 oz) sultanas or currants

175 ml (6 fl oz) Herb Dressing (see page 120)

1 Tear the lettuce into bite-sized pieces. Arrange them in a salad bowl. Peel the oranges and divide them into segments. Cut each segment into halves or thirds. Add the pieces to the salad bowl. Add the carrots and sultanas to the salad bowl and toss. Pour on the Cheese Herb Dressing and toss.

Mixed Green Garden Salad

Serves 6–8

1 head lettuce

1 medium-sized head Romaine lettuce

3 heads endive

stalk celery, chopped

100 g (4 oz) watercress, thick stems removed, coarsely chopped

½ medium-sized red onion, sliced into rings

20 cherry tomatoes, cut in half

24 black olives

2 tbsp fresh parsley, chopped

300 ml (10 fl oz) Rich Vinaigrette (see page 118)

1 Line the salad bowl with some leaves of the cabbage or garden lettuce.
2 Tear the remaining cabbage lettuce and the cos lettuce into bite-sized pieces. Add them to the salad bowl.
3 Cut the endive into bite-sized pieces. Add them to the salad bowl.
4 Add the celery, watercress, onion rings, tomatoes and olives to the salad bowl. Toss gently. Refrigerate until ready to serve.
5 Before serving, add the parsley and Rich Vinaigrette. Toss and serve.

Curly Endive and Alfalfa Sprouts Salad

Serves 4–6
½ small curly endive, torn into pieces
100 g (4 oz) alfalfa sprouts
50 g (2 oz) small button mushrooms, thinly sliced
½ red pepper, sliced

Dressing
juice 1 lemon
2 tsp olive oil
1 small onion, grated
¼ tsp Chinese five-spice powder

1   Arrange the curly endive on a large serving plate or four single plates.
2   Mix the alfalfa sprouts, mushrooms and pepper together in a bowl.
3   Mix the dressing ingredients together and add to the bowl of vegetables. Toss well and arrange on top of the lettuce.

California Waldorf Salad

Serves 6
90 g (3 oz) beansprouts or watercress
3 tart apples, cored and diced but not peeled
450 g (1 lb) celery, chopped
50 g (2 oz) flaked almonds
3 large mushrooms, coarsely chopped
250 ml (8 fl oz) Yogurt Mayonnaise
   (see page 115)
10 lettuce leaves
90 g (4 oz) seedless grapes, halved

1   Blanch the beansprouts in a saucepan of boiling water for 45 seconds. Drain and rinse in cold water. Drain well again. Coarsely chop the beansprouts.
2   Put the apple, celery, almonds and mushrooms in a large mixing bowl. Mix well with a wooden spoon.
3   Add the Yogurt Mayonnaise and mix thoroughly.
4   Line a serving platter with the lettuce leaves. Mound the beansprouts in the center. Transfer the mixed ingredients to the platter and garnish with the halved grapes.

Classic Waldorf Salad

Serves 2–4
8 stalks crisp celery
2 rosy-skinned dessert apples
handful of salad leaves, shredded
lemon juice
50 g (2 oz) walnuts
6 tbsp good mayonnaise
salt and freshly ground black pepper

1 If the celery is not crisp, immerse it in ice-cold water. It will soon freshen up. Pat dry and slice.
2 Core the apples but do not peel—the pink skin will give color contrast to the salad. Slice and sprinkle with lemon juice to prevent discoloring. Toss all the ingredients in the mayonnaise and season well.

Variation
This salad also tastes good with blue cheese dressing. Blend the mayonnaise with 1 tbsp blue cheese before adding to the salad.

Greek Salad

Serves 4
selection of salad leaves
20 cherry tomatoes, sliced
½ cucumber, thinly sliced
1 red onion, sliced
1 red pepper, sliced
handful black olives
175 g (6 oz) feta cheese, cubed
olive oil
salt and freshly ground black pepper

1 Combine the vegetables and cheese in a large bowl. Pour over enough olive oil to just coat the salad. Season well and toss.
2 Chill for an hour. Toss again, check seasoning and serve.

Strawberry and Avocado Salad

Serves 2
1 ripe avocado
175 g (6 oz) strawberries
1 tbsp strawberry vinegar
1 tbsp olive oil
freshly ground black pepper

1 Cut avocado in half lengthways and remove the pit. Carefully remove the flesh from the shell in one piece, using a metal spoon or pallet knife. Cut each half into slices and arrange around the edge of the serving plate.
2 Hull and slice the strawberries. Pile in the middle of the plate.
3 Mix together the strawberry vinegar and olive oil and pour over salad. Season with lots of black pepper.

Avocado and Grapefruit Salad

Serves 6
1 ripe avocado
2 tbsp fresh lemon juice
1 head romaine lettuce
700 g (1½ lb) seeded grapefruit segments
1 red onion, thinly sliced
250 ml (8 fl oz) Rich Vinaigrette (see page 118)

1 Peel the avocado and cut it into slices. Put the slices in a bowl and sprinkle with the lemon Juice.
2 Tear the lettuce into bite-sized pieces and arrange on the plates with the grapefruit, avocado and onion. Drizzle over the Rich Vinaigrette. Refrigerate for 30 minutes before serving.

Russian Radish and Cucumber Zakusky

Serves 4–6
2 hard-boiled eggs
250 ml (8 fl oz) sour cream
¾ tsp salt
1 tsp freshly ground black pepper
3 tbsp chopped fresh dill
225 g (8 oz) radishes, thinly sliced
1 large cucumber, peeled, seeded and
   thinly sliced

1 Remove the yolks from the eggs. Put them in a small mixing bowl and mash well with a fork. Chop the whites and set them aside.
2 Add the sour cream, salt, pepper and 2 tbsp of the dill to the mixing bowl. Stir until well blended.
3 Arrange the radishes and cucumber slices on a serving platter. Add the egg yolk and sour cream mixture. Garnish with the remaining dill and the chopped egg whites, and serve with black bread and small glasses of vodka in the Russian manner.

Summer Macaroni Salad

Serves 6–8

75 ml (6 fl oz) mayonnaise
2 tsp Dijon-style mustard
1 tbsp white wine vinegar
¼ tsp celery seeds
450 g (1 lb) macaroni, cooked
90 g (3 oz) celery, chopped
75 g (2½ oz) raw carrots, chopped
50 g (2 oz) radishes, sliced
3 tbsp chopped pimento-stuffed green olives
3 tbsp chopped red pepper
5 tbsp chopped scallions
2 tbsp chopped fresh parsley
¾ tsp salt
¼ tsp freshly ground black pepper

1 Put the mayonnaise, mustard, vinegar and celery
   seeds in a small mixing bowl. Beat with a fork or
   electric beater until well blended.
2 Put the macaroni in a large serving bowl and add
   the mayonnaise mixture. Toss until the macaroni
   is well coated. Add the celery, carrots, radishes,
   olives, red peppers, scallions and parsley. Toss
   well. Add the salt and pepper. Toss lightly.
3 Cover the bowl and chill for 1½ hours. Remove
   from the fridge and serve.

Coleslaw

Serves 6

1 small head crisp white cabbage
½ head red cabbage
2 carrots, grated
2 tbsp chives, chopped
50 g (2 oz) sultanas
1 tbsp sesame seeds
Mayonnaise (see page 114)

1 Shred the cabbage finely, discarding the stalk.
   Grate the carrots.
2 Toss all the ingredients together in the
   Mayonnaise and mix well. Taste and adjust
   seasoning. Chill overnight in the fridge. Mix well
   again before serving.

Double Gloucester Salad

Serves 2

100 g (4 oz) Double Gloucester cheese
2 handfuls young spinach leaves
1 bunch watercress
2 large tomatoes
50 g (2 oz) mushrooms
6–8 scallions
2 tbsp olive oil
1 tbsp wine vinegar
1–2 tsp mustard powder
salt and freshly ground black pepper

1 Cube the cheese. Wash the spinach and watercress, discarding stalks and any tough or yellow leaves. Immerse the tomatoes in boiling water until their skins split, then refresh with cold water, peel and roughly chop. Slice the mushrooms. Trim the scallions; make several lengthways cuts around each into the onion and splay out the layers in a decorative fashion.
2 Make the dressing by combining the oil, vinegar, mustard powder and seasoning.
3 Combine the watercress, spinach, tomatoes and mushrooms in a salad bowl, add the dressing and toss. Top with the cheese and onions.

Middle-Eastern Coleslaw

Serves 4–6

700 g (1½ lb) cabbage, ¼ tsp sugar
   coarsely grated ½ tsp honey
2–3 tbsp salt 1 tsp chili flakes
250 ml (8 fl oz) fresh 2 tsp white
   orange juice   wine vinegar
3 tbs fresh lemon juice ½ tsp salt

1 Put the grated cabbage in a colander. Sprinkle the 2 to 3 tbsp of salt over the cabbage and let it stand for 1 hour.
2 Rinse the salt from the cabbage. Drain. Wrap the cabbage in a paper towel and squeeze as much liquid from it as possible.
3 Put the orange juice, lemon juice, sugar, honey, chili flakes, vinegar and salt in a salad bowl. Stir until mixed. Add the cabbage to the salad bowl and toss well.

Cauliflower, Blue Cheese and Yogurt Salad

Serves 4

1 head cauliflower
4 tbsp yogurt
2 tbsp blue cheese, softened
4 tbsp parsley, chopped
salt and freshly ground black pepper

1 Cut the cauliflower into tiny florets—reserve the stalks for use in a soup.
2 Cream the yogurt and blue cheese together. Toss cauliflower and parsley in the dressing and season well.

Potato Salad with Horseradish

Serves 4
700 g (1½ lb) new potatoes
150 ml (5 fl oz) sour cream
3 tbsp finely grated horseradish
pinch paprika
½ tsp honey
salt and freshly ground black pepper
bunch scallions
chives
handful chopped parsley

1 Wash the potatoes, but do not peel. Boil in salted water until tender.
2 Meanwhile, make the dressing. Combine the sour cream with the horseradish, paprika and honey. Mix well and season with salt and pepper.
3 Trim the scallions and slit down the stems so that they curl outwards. Chop the chives.
4 When the potatoes are done, slice them while still hot and mix into the dressing with the parsley. Toss in the onions or chives. Serve immediately, or chill and serve cold.

Traditional Potato Salad

Serves 4–6
700 g (1½ lb) new potatoes, cooked and diced
1 medium-sized red onion, finely chopped
225 g (8 oz) celery, sliced
2 hard-boiled eggs, chopped
175 ml (6 fl oz) mayonnaise
2 tbsp wine vinegar
½ tsp salt
1 tsp finely ground black pepper
2 tbsp chopped fresh parsley

1 In a salad bowl, put the potatoes, onion, celery and eggs. Mix lightly.
2 Add the mayonnaise, vinegar, salt and pepper. Toss to coat all the ingredients. Garnish with parsley and serve.

German Potato Salad

Serves 6
6 large potatoes or 900 g (2 lb) small potatoes
4 scallions, finely chopped
1 garlic clove, finely chopped
1 tsp capers, drained
2 tbsp fresh dill, chopped
2 tbsp chopped fresh parsley
1 tsp salt
1 tsp freshly ground black pepper
4 tbsp olive oil
3 tbsp white wine vinegar
1 tbsp vegetable stock (optional)
½ tsp sugar

1 Cook the potatoes, in their skins, in a large pot of lightly salted boiling water. Drain well, peel while warm and dice. (Leave small potatoes whole and unpeeled, if you prefer).
2 Put the potatoes in a salad bowl and add the scallions, garlic, capers, dill and parsley. Toss lightly.
3 Into a jar with a tightly fitting lid, put the salt, pepper, olive oil, vinegar, vegetable stock and sugar. Cover and shake until blended.
4 Pour the dressing over the potato salad and toss lightly. Let it stand at room temperature for 1½ hours before serving.

Italian Zucchini Salad

Serves 4
2 medium-sized zucchini
8 tbsp olive oil
3 tbsp red wine vinegar
1 scallion, white part only, finely chopped
½ tsp dried basil
⅛ tsp/large pinch dried oregano
⅛ tsp/large pinch dried marjoram
1 garlic clove, crushed
¼ tsp salt
2 tbsp chopped fresh parsley
½ tsp freshly ground black pepper

1 Cook the zucchini in a pot of salted boiling water for 7 to 8 minutes. Drain well and rinse in very cold water for 5 minutes. Drain again. Slice them thinly.
2 Put the olive oil, vinegar, scallion, basil, oregano, marjoram, garlic and salt in a jar with a tightly fitting lid. Cover tightly and shake until well blended.
3 Put the zucchini and the dressing in a salad bowl. Toss very gently. Let it stand for 15 to 20 minutes. Sprinkle with parsley and pepper and serve.

51

Pulses and Feta Cheese Salad

Serves 4

350 g (12 oz) brown pulses
1 bay leaf
½ tsp dried basil
2 garlic cloves, crushed
stalk celery, finely chopped
1 small onion, chopped
3 tbsp fresh chives, chopped
175 g (6 oz) feta cheese, crumbled
6 tbsp extra-virgin olive oil
3 tbsp red wine vinegar
⅛ tsp/large pinch dried oregano
salt and freshly ground black pepper

1 Put the pulses in a bowl. Add 750 ml (1¼ pt) cold water and soak the pulses for 2 hours. Drain.
2 Put the pulses in a saucepan and add enough cold water to cover them completely. Add the bay leaf, basil and 1 garlic clove. Bring to a boil and simmer, covered, for 20 minutes.
3 Add the celery and onion. Add enough additional water to cover the pulses. Cover the saucepan and simmer for 10 more minutes.
4 Drain the pulses, celery and onion and discard the bay leaf and garlic clove. Put the pulses, celery and onion in a serving bowl. Add the chives and feta cheese. Toss.
5 Put the olive oil, vinegar, oregano, remaining garlic clove, salt and pepper in a jar with a tightly fitting lid. Cover tightly and shake until well blended.
6 Pour the dressing over the salad and toss. Let the salad stand for 2 hours, tossing occasionally, before serving.

Egg and Pasta Salad

Serves 4

225 g (8 oz) green or wholewheat pasta shapes
2 tsp oil
4 eggs
100 g (4 oz) green beans
2 stalks celery
1 dessert apple
50 g (2 oz) walnuts
Mayonnaise (see page 114)
salt and freshly ground black pepper
1–2 tbsp dill

1 Cook the pasta in plenty of boiling salted water, to which you have added oil, until al dente. Drain and leave to cool.
2 Hard-boil the eggs, peel under cold running water and leave to cool. Cut into quarters.
3 Top and tail the beans and cut into manageable lengths. Simmer in salted water until cooked but not soft. Drain and leave to cool.
4 Chop the celery. Peel, core and dice the apple. Toss all the ingredients except the eggs together in the Mayonnaise. Season and garnish with eggs and dill.

Navy Bean Salad

Serves 4

175 g (6 oz) dried navy beans, soaked overnight	salt and freshly ground black pepper
2 cloves garlic, crushed	1 red pepper, seeded and thinly sliced
2 tbsp red wine vinegar	1 leek, thinly sliced
2 tbsp olive oil	2 scallions, green and white parts chopped separately
1 tsp Dijon mustard	

1. Place the beans in a large saucepan and cook with fresh water. Bring to a boil and boil vigorously for 10 minutes, then cover and simmer for 40–50 minutes or until tender. Drain.
2. Combine the garlic, vinegar, olive oil, mustard and seasoning in a screw-top jar, seal and shake well.
3. Pour over the hot beans and leave to cool. Stir in the pepper, leek and white parts of the scallions and place in a serving dish.
4. Sprinkle with green chopped onions and serve.

Barbecue Salad

Serves 4
3 large tomatoes, quartered
2 large green peppers, seeded and quartered
1 red pepper, seeded and quartered
1 large eggplant, peeled and quartered
2 large onions, halved
250 ml (8 fl oz) Herb Dressing (see page 120)

1   Thread the tomato, green pepper, red pepper and eggplant quarters and the onion halves onto 6 (or more) long skewers.
2   Lay the skewers on the grill over white coals or place them under a broiler at high heat. Cook for 12 to 15 minutes, turning frequently.
3   Remove the skewers from the grill. Remove the vegetables from the skewers. Put the eggplant and tomato pieces in a bowl.
4   While still hot, peel the skin from the pepper pieces. Add the pieces to the salad bowl. Coarsely chop the onions and add them to the salad bowl. Add the Herb Dressing and toss. Refrigerate for 30 minutes before serving.

Kidney Bean, Chickpea and Corn Salad

Serves 4
175 g (6 oz) kidney beans
175 g (6 oz) chickpeas
175 g (6 oz) corn, cooked
6 scallions
2 very large tomatoes
Herb Dressing (see page 120)

1   Soak the kidney beans and the chickpeas separately overnight, then simmer in water until cooked. Drain and cool. Add in the sweetcorn.
2   Chop the scallions and slice the tomatoes.
3   Toss all the ingredients in Herb Dressing and serve at room temperature with hot pita bread.

Green Bean and Pepper Salad

Serves 4

225 g (8 oz) green beans
1 medium or 2 small red peppers, cored and seeded
2 slices fresh ginger, thinly grated
1½ tsp salt
1 tsp sugar
1 tbsp sesame oil

1 Wash the green beans, snip off the ends and cut into 5 cm (2 in) lengths. Cut the red peppers into thin shreds. Blanch them both in boiling water and drain.
2 Put the green beans, red peppers and ginger into a bowl. Add the salt, sugar and sesame seed oil. Toss well and serve.

Tomato Salad with Scallion and Oil Dressing

Serves 4

275 g (10 oz) tomatoes, firm and not over-ripe
1 tsp salt
1 tsp sugar
3–4 scallions, finely chopped
3 tbsp oil

1 Wash and dry the tomatoes. Cut them into thick slices. Sprinkle with salt and sugar. Leave to marinate for 10–15 minutes.
2 Place the finely chopped scallions in a heat-resistant bowl. In a saucepan, heat the oil until quite hot and pour over the scallions. Add the tomatoes, toss well and serve.

Cook's Tip
Other vegetables such as cucumber, celery and green peppers can be served in the same manner.

Celery Salad

Serves 4
1 head celery
1 tsp salt
1.7 l (3½ pts) water
2 tbsp light soy sauce
1 tbsp vinegar
1 tbsp sesame oil
2 slices fresh ginger, finely grated

1 Remove the leaves and tough outer stalks of the celery. Thinly slice the tender parts diagonally. Blanch them in a saucepan of boiling, salted water. Then pour them into a colander and rinse in cold water until cool. Drain.
2 Mix together the soy sauce, vinegar and sesame oil. Add to the celery and toss well.
3 Garnish the salad with finely grated fresh ginger and serve.

Beansprout Salad

Serves 4
450 g (1 lb) fresh beansprouts
1 tsp salt
2.3 l (5 pts) water
2 tbsp light soy sauce
1 tbsp vinegar
Sesame oil
2 scallions, finely chopped

1 Wash and rinse the beansprouts in cold water, discarding the husks and other pieces that float to the surface. It is not necessary to trim each sprout.
2 Blanch the sprouts in a saucepan of salted, boiling water. Pour them into a colander and rinse in cold water until cool. Drain.
3 Place the sprouts in a bowl or a deep dish and add the soy sauce, vinegar and sesame oil. Toss well and garnish with finely chopped scallion just before serving.

Sweet and Sour Cucumber Salad

Serves 4
1 cucumber
2 tsp finely chopped fresh ginger
1 tsp sesame oil
2 tbsp sugar
2 tbsp rice vinegar

1 Select a dark green and slender cucumber; the fat pale green ones contain too much water and have far less flavor. Cut it in half lengthways, then cut each piece into slices. Marinate with the ginger and sesame oil for about 10–15 minutes.
2 Make the dressing with the sugar and vinegar in a bowl, stirring well to dissolve the sugar.
3 Place the cucumber slices on a plate. Just before serving, pour the sugar and vinegar dressing evenly over them and toss well.

Caribbean Fruit Salad

Serves 6–8

225 g (8 oz) blueberries or blackcurrants

2 peaches, stoned and thinly sliced

225 g (8 oz) green and black seedless grapes, halved

225 g (8 oz) fresh pineapple chunks

225 g (8 oz) diced honeydew melon

5 tangerines, peeled, white membrane removed, segmented and seeded

225 g (8 oz) diced cantaloupe

225 g (8 oz) cubed Gruyère cheese

225 g (8 oz) fresh dates

1 tbsp honey

2 tbsp rum

250 ml (8 fl oz) Yogurt Mayonnaise (see page 115)

2 large bananas, halved

90 g (3 oz) finely chopped almonds

1 Arrange the blueberries, peaches, grapes, pineapple, honeydew melon, tangerines, cantaloupe melon, cheese and dates on a large platter.

2 In a small mixing bowl, add the honey and rum to the Yogurt mayonnaise and stir until well mixed. Place the dressing in a separate bowl in the center of the platter.

3 Lightly roll the banana pieces in the chopped almonds and add them to the rest of the fruit.

4 Let each guest take some fruit and dress their own portion.

South Seas Fruit Salad

Serves 6–8

2 ripe papayas, peeled, seeded and cubed

2 large bananas, peeled and diced

90 g (3 oz) seedless green grapes, halved

225 g (8 oz) cubed pineapple

3 tangerines, peeled, white membrane removed, segmented and seeded

5 tbsp peanut oil

1 tbsp sesame oil

4 tbsp fresh lime juice

¼ tsp salt

2 tsp sugar

1 Arrange the papaya, banana, grapes, pineapple and tangerine segments in serving bowls.

2 Into a blender or food processor, put the peanut oil, sesame oil, lime juice, salt and sugar. Blend until well mixed.

3 Pour the dressing over the salad. Cover the bowls and chill for 1 to 2 hours before serving.

Pear Salad

Serves 4

4 pears
1 clove garlic, crushed
1 tsp salt
1½ tsp sugar
½ tsp dried tarragon, crumbled
½ tsp dried basil, crumbled
2½ tbsp red wine vinegar
2½ tbsp olive oil
2½ tbsp water
1 tbsp sherry
100 g (4 oz) celery, coarsely chopped
100 g (4 oz) green pepper, coarsely chopped
3 scallions, sliced
2 large ripe tomatoes, finely chopped
4 romaine lettuce leaves, chilled

1 Wash the pears and refrigerate. In a bowl mix together the garlic, salt and sugar. Add the tarragon, basil, vinegar, oil, water and sherry. Whisk until well blended. Transfer to a ½ l (16 fl oz) jar, cover, and leave stand for 1 to 1½ hours.
2 Place the celery, green pepper, scallions and tomatoes in a bowl. Chill for 1 hour.
3 Remove the vegetables and pears from the fridge. Shake the dressing to mix well. Pour half the dressing over the vegetables and toss.
4 Place 1 lettuce leaf on each of four serving plates. Halve and core the pears. Arrange 2 pear halves, cut-side up, on each lettuce leaf. Top with the dressed vegetables. Spoon the remaining dressing over the pears and serve.

Melon Salad with Ginger Sauce

Serves 6–8

175 ml (6 fl oz) whipping cream
1 tsp fresh lemon juice
1 tbsp powdered sugar
large pinch cayenne pepper
3 large pieces preserved ginger, finely chopped
50 g (2 oz) almonds, chopped
2 large melons of your choice, peeled, seeded and cubed

1 Put the cream, lemon juice, sugar and cayenne pepper in a mixing bowl. Beat or whisk the cream until it becomes thick but not stiff. Add the ginger and the almonds, reserving 1 tbsp of the almonds. Continue to beat or whisk until the cream becomes stiff. Cover the bowl and chill until ready to serve.
2 Put the melon in a serving dish and chill until ready to serve. Just before serving, top the melon cubes with the ginger. Sprinkle the remaining almonds on top.

PASTA AND CREPE DISHES

Tasty and filling, pasta is a much-loved favorite, for the youngest to the most sophisticated diner. Available in myriad shapes and sizes, it is exceptionally versatile and does service as a first course, luncheon special, main dish or party piece. Crêpes may require more preparation, but the results are always delectable.

Asparagus Crêpes

Serves 2
1 small clove garlic, crushed
2 tbsp fresh basil leaves, chopped
1 tbsp pinenuts
3 tbsp Parmesan cheese, grated
2 tbsp olive oil
salt and freshly ground black pepper
crêpes (see page 61)
200 g (7 oz) asparagus spears
3 tomatoes, skinned, seeded and chopped

1   Place the garlic, basil, pinenuts and 2 tbsp Parmesan cheese in a food processor or blender and purée. With the motor running, gradually add the oil and blend into a smooth sauce. Season to taste.
2   Place the flours in a bowl, and gradually add the egg and milk, beating well to form a smooth batter.
3   Make the crêpes and keep warm (see page 61).
4   Place the asparagus in a saucepan, pour over just enough boiling water to cover and simmer for 6 minutes.
5   Divide the asparagus between the crêpes, top with sauce and fold up. Place in a shallow ovenproof dish, and sprinkle with the tomatoes and remaining cheese.
6   Place under the broiler until browned.

Mushroom Crêpes

Serves 4
crêpes, cooked on 1 side (see page 61)
2 tbsp butter
1 large onion, finely chopped
450 g (1 lb) mushrooms, chopped
2 tbsp canned red pimentos, finely chopped
150 ml (¼ pt) sour cream, plus more to serve
salt and freshly ground black pepper
melted butter

1   Make the crêpes and keep warm (see page 61).
2   Melt the butter and add the onion, cook until the onion has softened but not browned. Add the mushrooms and cook until soft. Drain off any excess liquid.
3   Mix in the pimentoes, sour cream, salt and pepper.
4   Spoon the mixture onto each of the crêpes on the cooked side, and roll each crêpe tucking in the edges.
5   Place the rolled crêpes in a buttered oven dish and drizzle a little melted butter over the top. Warm through in the over at 180°C/350°F/Gas Mark 4 for 25 minutes.
6   Serve with chilled sour cream (if desired).

Crêpes

Serves 4 (Makes 1.1 l (2 pt))
600 ml (1 pt) milk
225 g (8 oz) flour
pinch salt
2 eggs
butter or oil for frying

1   Mix the milk and flour together until smooth. Add the salt and eggs and beat in well.
2   Heat a little butter or oil in a heavy-based saucepan (preferably one used only for crêpes). Pour out excess butter.
3   Pour in just enough batter to coat the bottom of the saucepan. Fry on one side only if the crêpes are to be filled.

Stuffed Cheese Crêpes

Serves 3–4
40 g (1½ oz) all-purpose flour
40 g (1½ oz) whole wheat flour
pinch salt
1 egg
150 ml (5 fl oz) milk
1 tbsp melted butter

Cheese and herb filling
450 g (1 lb) cottage cheese
2 tbsp half and half
1 large clove garlic, crushed
2 tbsp fresh herbs, finely chopped
1 tbsp scallion, chopped

1 To make the crêpe mixture, sift the flour and salt into a bowl. Make a well in the middle of it and add the egg. Gradually beat in the milk. When half of the milk has been added, beat in the melted butter. Continue beating in the milk until you have a thin batter. Allow the batter to stand for half an hour.
2 Meanwhile, prepare the filling. Combine the cottage cheese with the rest of the ingredients and mix well.
3 Make the crêpes and leave to cool (see page 61).
4 Divide the filling between them, rolling the crêpes around it into a cigar shape. Arrange the stuffed crêpes in an ovenproof dish and heat in a moderate oven for about 1½ minutes.

Fettucini Romana

Serves 4
Oil
pinch salt
450 g (1 lb) fettucini
4 tbsp/50 g (2 oz) butter
½ tsp ground nutmeg
150 ml (¼ pt) half and half
salt and freshly ground black pepper
100 g (4 oz) Parmesan cheese

1 Bring a well-filled saucepan of salted water to a boil, and add a few drops of oil and salt. Feed in the fettucini and cook until al dente (fresh pasta will only take about 2 minutes). Drain in a colander.
2 Melt the butter in the saucepan, and add ground nutmeg. Pour in half of the cream and stir until shiny and bubbles start to appear. Season with salt and pepper.
3 Add the fettucini and stir around in the saucepan. Pour in the remaining cream and cheese alternately, forking the pasta as it is mixed. Serve immediately.

Cook's Tip
This is a real pasta lovers' dish. For the best results use freshly grated Parmesan cheese rather than the ready grated variety.

Genoese Pasta with Pesto Sauce

Serves 4–6

2 tbsp fresh basil leaves

2 cloves garlic

100 ml (4 fl oz) olive oil

50 g (2 oz) pinenuts

50 g (2 oz) Parmesan cheese

pinch salt

2 tbsp butter

450 g (1 lb) spaghetti or tagliatelle, cooked
   and drained

1 Blend the basil leaves in a blender. Add the crushed cloves of garlic and olive oil. Process for a few seconds.

2 Gradually add the pine kernels, Parmesan cheese, and season, remembering that Parmesan has a salty taste. The consistency should be thick and creamy.

3 Melt the butter in the saucepan and add the cooked pasta to reheat. Remove from the heat and mix 2 tbsp pesto with the pasta. Serve on individual plates with a spoonful of pesto on each helping. Garnish with more grated Parmesan.

Eggplant and Apple Pasta

Serves 2–3
1 large eggplant
salt and freshly ground black pepper
1 large cooking apple
1 egg, beaten
seasoned all-purpose flour (enough to
    coat the eggplant)
4 tbsp walnut oil
2 cloves garlic, crushed
225 g (8 oz) wholewheat or spinach
    pasta shells
Parmesan cheese, grated

1 Slice the eggplant, sprinkle liberally with salt and leave in a colander for 30 minutes. Rinse and dry on paper towels and cut into strips. Peel, core and dice the apple.
2 Toss the eggplant and apple in the beaten egg, and then in the seasoned flour to give a light coating. Heat some walnut oil in a saucepan and fry the eggplant, apple and garlic, stirring, until crisp.
3 Meanwhile, cook pasta shells in plenty of salted water at a full rolling boil, until al dente. Add a few drops of oil to the water to prevent the pasta from sticking. Drain well, season with black pepper and toss in a little walnut oil. Stir in the eggplant mixture and serve with Parmesan cheese.

Spinach Tagliatelle with Asparagus

Serves 2
6–7 spears asparagus
2 tbsp butter
4 tbsp/60 ml (2 fl oz) half and half
salt and freshly ground black pepper
225 g (8 oz) spinach tagliatelle
2 tsp oil
Parmesan cheese, grated

1 If you are using fresh asparagus, clean it under cold running water, tie it in a bundle and stand upright in a tall saucepan containing about 7 cm (3 in) boiling salted water. Cover with foil so that the asparagus tips cook by steaming. Alternatively, use a bowl over a saucepan of simmering water, inverting the inner saucepan over the bottom one. The asparagus will take 10–20 minutes to cook, depending on its thickness. (Test by piercing halfway up the stalk with a sharp knife—if you can insert the knife easily, the asparagus is done). Drain it. Cut off and discard the woody lower pieces. Cut the asparagus into bite-sized pieces.
2 Melt the butter in a saucepan and toss the asparagus in it. Add half the cream, season and leave for a few minutes over a very low heat to thicken.
3 Meanwhile, cook the pasta until al dente in plenty of boiling salted water to which you have added 2 tsp oil.
4 Drain the pasta, toss in the remaining cream and pour over the asparagus sauce. Serve and offer a generous amount of Parmesan cheese.

Spinach and Ricotta Pasta

Serves 6–8

300 ml (½ pt) Béchamel Sauce (page 116)
225 g (8 oz) (after cooking) fresh or
  frozen spinach
100 g (4 oz) ricotta cheese
salt and freshly ground pepper
½ tsp nutmeg
500–750 g (1–1½ lb) cooked pasta

1 Make the Béchamel sauce.
2 Cook the spinach for a few minutes and then drain well. Squeeze against the colander to remove the liquid.
3 You will need to cook approx 750 g (1½ lb) fresh spinach to be left with the amount required by the recipe. Chop or blend.
4 Mix the ricotta with the spinach and season well, add nutmeg. Gradually stir into the Béchamel Sauce and reheat carefully over low heat. Serve in spoonfuls over portions of the cooked pasta.

Spaghetti Puttanesca

Serves 4–6

1 onion, peeled and diced
2 tbsp oil
2 cloves garlic, crushed
1 carrot, peeled and chopped
400 g (14 oz) canned tomatoes
2 tomatoes, skinned and chopped
4 tbsp white wine
1 bay leaf
3–4 basil leaves or 1 tsp dried basil
salt and freshly ground black pepper
2 tbsp capers, chopped
50 g (2 oz) black olives, stoned
3 drops Tabasco
1 tbsp fresh parsley, chopped
450 g (1 lb) cooked spaghetti
Parmesan cheese, grated, to serve

1 Put the onion into the oil in a large frying pan over low heat. Cook gently for 4 minutes, then add the crushed garlic and carrot. Turn in the oil twice more.
2 Add the tomatoes, white wine, bay leaf, basil and some seasoning. Bring to a boil and simmer for 30 minutes. Sieve or blend and return the sauce to the saucepan. Add the chopped capers, chopped olives and the Tabasco sauce. Reheat and serve over the cooked spaghetti, with Parmesan cheese.

Tagliatelle with Sweet Pepper Sauce

Serves 4
1 small red pepper
1 small green pepper
1 small yellow pepper
salt and freshly ground black pepper
1–2 tbsp olive oil
1 onion, chopped
2 cloves garlic, chopped
400 g (15 oz) canned tomatoes
1 tbsp tomato paste
fresh basil leaves, snipped
350 g (12 oz) spinach tagliatelle
Parmesan cheese, grated

1 Trim and de-seed the peppers and cut into narrow strips. You can make the sauce with green peppers alone if you wish, but the red and yellow varieties are sweeter and make the dish look more colorful. Blanch the peppers for a minute in boiling salted water, refresh in cold water, then drain.
2 Heat the olive oil in a saucepan, add the garlic and onions and cook gently, stirring, until soft. Add the tomatoes, tomato paste and basil. Break up the tomatoes with a wooden spoon and simmer for about 5 minutes. Season to taste and blend the sauce in a blender. Return to the saucepan over a very low heat and add the peppers.
3 Cook the pasta in a large saucepan with plenty of water to which you have added a little oil and salt. The water should be at a full rolling boil. The pasta will be ready in about 9 minutes. Drain and divide between single warmed serving bowls.
4 Spoon the sauce over each helping of pasta and serve at once with Parmesan cheese.

Vegetarian Bolognese Sauce

Serves 4–6
225 g (8 oz) brown pulses
salt and freshly ground black pepper
1 bay leaf
1–2 tbsp olive oil
1 onion, chopped
2 cloves garlic, chopped
1 carrot, chopped
1 stick celery, chopped
400 g (15 oz) canned tomatoes, mashed
1 tbsp tomato paste
½ tsp dried mixed herbs
2 tbsp red wine
350 g (12 oz) wholewheat or spinach pasta

1 Soak the pulses overnight and simmer in salted water with a bay leaf until they can be mashed with a fork. Drain and discard the bay leaf.
2 Heat the oil in a saucepan and fry the onion and garlic until translucent. Add the carrot and celery and cook for a further 2 minutes.
3 Add the tomatoes and a little juice. Add the remaining ingredients and the pulses. Simmer until the sauce is quite thick. Blend or partially blend in a blender.
4 Serve the sauce in healthy spoonfuls over the warmed cooked pasta.

Pasta with Mushroom Sauce

Serves 1–2
2–4 handfuls spinach pasta spirals
salt and freshly ground black pepper
1 tsp oil
50 g (2 oz) mushrooms
milk
1 egg yolk
1 tbsp half and half
parsley, chopped
Parmesan cheese, grated

1   Cook the pasta in plenty of boiling salted water with 1 tsp oil, until al dente.
2   Meanwhile, wipe and slice the mushrooms. Place in a saucepan with a little milk, season well and poach gently, stirring, until soft and very black and the liquid has almost gone.
3   Beat the egg yolk with the cream and stir in the mushrooms.
4   Drain the pasta and stir in the mushroom mixture with plenty of parsley. Serve at once with Parmesan and a tender lettuce salad.

Spaghetti with Mascarpone

Serves 4
350 g (12 oz) wholewheat spaghetti
salt and freshly ground black pepper
a little oil
2 egg yolks
100 g (4 oz) mascarpone or cream cheese
grated Parmesan cheese to serve

1   Cook the pasta in boiling salted water, to which you have added a few drops of oil, until al dente.
2   While you are draining the spaghetti, stir the egg yolks and mascarpone together in a large saucepan over a low heat.
3   When the sauce begins to set, toss in the spaghetti. Serve at once with plenty of black pepper and Parmesan. This dish should be accompanied by a crunchy salad.

Hot Pasta Salad

Serves 4
2 cloves garlic
3 tbsp olive oil
handful fresh basil leaves
1 tbsp Parmesan cheese, grated

The salad
100 g (4 oz) mozzarella cheese
450 g (1 lb) plum tomatoes
75 g (3 oz) black olives
salt and freshly ground black pepper

The pasta
350 g (12 oz) spinach pasta twists
1 tsp olive oil

1   Chop the garlic and put it in a mortar. Pour in a little of the olive oil and pound it into a pulp. Gradually add the basil leaves and cheese with the rest of the oil, pounding all the time. You should have a thick paste.
2   Dice the mozzarella. Peel the tomatoes by immersing them in boiling water until their skins burst. Chop them roughly. Mix the cheese, tomatoes and olives together and season.
3   Cook the pasta in boiling salted water, to which you have added a little olive oil, until al dente. Drain. Toss the pasta in the dressing. Pile it into four warmed serving bowls and top with the salad.

Spaghetti with Fresh Tomato and Basil Sauce

Serves 4
2 tsp olive oil
1 onion, chopped
4 stalks celery, chopped
1 green chili, seeded and finely chopped
2 cloves garlic, crushed
700 g (1½ lb) tomatoes, skinned and
    roughly chopped
3 tbsp tomato paste
1 tbsp basil leaves, chopped
1 tbsp marjoram, chopped
350 g (12 oz) wholewheat spaghetti or
    175 g (6 oz) wholewheat spaghetti and
    175 g (6 oz) spinach spaghetti
50 g (2 oz) black olives, pitted
3 tbsp Parmesan cheese, grated
3 tbsp pinenuts
basil sprigs

1   Heat the oil in a saucepan, add the onion, celery, chili and garlic and fry until soft. Add the tomatoes and tomato paste, 4 tbsp water, half the basil and marjoram. Bring to a boil and simmer for 10 minutes.
2   Place the wholewheat spaghetti in a large saucepan of boiling, lightly salted water and cook for 12 minutes, or until just tender. Add the spinach spaghetti, if using, 2 minutes after the wholewheat spaghetti.
3   Drain the pasta and divide between four single warmed plates. Stir the olives and remaining basil into the sauce and place on top of the spaghetti.
4   Sprinkle with cheese and nuts, garnish with basil sprigs and serve.

MAIN COURSES

Vegetarian main courses should appeal as much to everyday meat eaters as to herbivore gourmets. These cosmopolitan combinations of vegetables, cheeses, herbs and spices result in dishes that are full in flavor and varied in texture, whether they are a healthy family lunch or a light supper.

Endive Soufflé

Serves 4–6

3 heads endive
salt
juice of 1 lemon
3 tbsp butter
40 g (1½ oz) flour
300 ml (10 fl oz) milk
50 g (2 oz) grated cheese
4 eggs, separated
1 tbsp dry brown breadcrumbs

1 Heat the oven to 200°C/400°F/Gas Mark 6. Trim the endive and cook in salted water, to which you have added the lemon juice. This will stop it discoloring.

2 When the endive is tender, drain and set aside. When it is cool, press the water out from between the leaves with your fingers. Chop the endive very finely.

3 Meanwhile, melt the butter in a heavy-bottomed saucepan. Stir in the flour. Remove from the heat and stir in the milk. Return to the heat and stir until the sauce has thickened. Add the cheese and cook for one more minute. Leave to cool.

4 When the sauce has cooled, mix in the endive, then the egg yolks.

5 Whisk the whites until they form soft peaks, and fold into the endive mixture. Spoon into a greased soufflé dish and sprinkle the top with breadcrumbs.

6 Bake in the oven for 20–25 minutes until lightly set, well risen and golden on top. Serve this soufflé with a strongly flavored salad, such as watercress garnished with slivers of orange.

Spinach and Cheese Soufflé

Serves 4

450 g (1 lb) spinach, washed and picked over
4 tbsp butter or margarine
50 g (2 oz) flour
450 ml (15 fl oz) milk
6 eggs
225 g (8 oz) cottage cheese
grated nutmeg
salt and freshly ground black pepper
grated Parmesan (optional)

1 Cook the spinach without any excess water. Drain it very well (between two plates is the most effective way).
2 While the spinach is cooking, melt the butter and stir in the flour off the heat. Slowly add the milk and return the saucepan to the heat. Stir to thicken the sauce. Remove the saucepan from the heat.
3 Separate the eggs and add the yolks, one at a time, mixing after each one. Add the cooked and drained spinach, cottage cheese, nutmeg, salt and pepper to taste. Mix everything together well.
4 Whisk the whites until they are very stiff. Take a scoop of this and fold it gently into the spinach mixture to lighten it a little and then incorporate the rest of the egg-whites into it, mixing it in lightly. Pour the soufflé mixture into a greased soufflé dish measuring about 21 x 9 cm (8¼ x 3½ in). Bake at 190°C/375°F/Gas Mark 5 for 30 minutes. Test with a clean knife to see if it is ready. If the mixture is still very runny, return the dish to the oven for a further 5 minutes or so. If you like, sprinkle some grated Parmesan on the top 10 minutes before the end of cooking.

Savory Pumpkin Tart

Serves 4–6

1 recipe Wholewheat Pastry (see page 147)
450 g (1 lb) pumpkin flesh
4 eggs
150 ml (5 fl oz) whipping cream
150 ml (5 fl oz) milk
2 large tomatoes, peeled and chopped
1 tbsp chopped fresh basil leaves
freshly ground black pepper

1 Make the pastry as directed on page 147. Roll out and line a greased 22 cm (8 in) quiche pan.
2 Preheat the oven to 190°C/375°F/Gas Mark 5.
3 Remove the rind and seeds from the pumpkin and cut into slivers. Pack into a saucepan with very little water and cook over low heat, covered. Check the saucepan occasionally to make sure the pumpkin hasn't dried out. After about 20 minutes you should be able to mash it into a purée.
4 Beat the eggs with the cream and milk. Mix in the pumpkin, tomato and basil and pour into the crust. Bake for 45 minutes until set and golden.

Onion Tart

Serves 4–6

175 g (6 oz) shortcrust pastry (enough for a
single-crust pie) (see page 147)

1 tbsp butter

1 tbsp olive oil

550 g (1 lb) finely chopped onions

2 eggs plus 1 yolk

450 ml (15 fl oz) half and half

1–2 heaped tbsp grated Cheddar cheese

1–2 heaped tbsp chopped parsley

salt and freshly ground black pepper

pinch of cayenne pepper

1 Heat the oven to 375°F/190°C/Gas Mark 5 and
line a 22 cm (8 in) quiche tin with the pastry.

2 Heat the butter and olive oil in a saucepan. Stir
in the onions. Cover the saucepan, turn down
the heat and sweat for about 5 minutes, stirring
occasionally until soft and transparent.

3 Beat the eggs, cream and cheese together and
add the onions and parsley. Season with salt,
pepper and cayenne to taste, pour into the pastry
crust and bake in the middle of the oven for
30–40 minutes until golden and set.

Variation

To make an onion and blue cheese tart, combine
1–2 tbsp crumbled blue cheese with the cream before
beating it with the eggs. Omit the Cheddar, parsley
and cayenne pepper.

Leek Quiche

Serves 4–6
20 cm (8 in) pie plate lined with pastry
butter
450 g (1 lb) leeks, trimmed and chopped
1 large onion, chopped
225 g (8 oz) cottage cheese
3 eggs
salt and freshly ground black pepper
pinch of ground mixed spice

1 Bake the pastry case for 10 minutes at
   350°F/180°C/Gas Mark 4.
2 Heat the butter and soften the leeks and onion in
   it for 5 minutes. Mix the cottage cheese with the
   remaining ingredients.
3 Cover the bottom of the lined pie plate with the
   cooked leeks and onions. Spoon over the cottage
   cheese mixture. Bake at 180°C/350°F/Gas Mark 4
   for 35 minutes. Serve hot or at room temperature.

Green Pea Tartlets with Poached Eggs

Makes 8 tartlets
250 g (8 oz) shortcrust pastry (enough for
   a single-crust pie) (see page 147)
900 g (2 lb) peas
4 tbsp butter
salt and freshly ground black pepper
8 eggs

Tomato sauce
1–2 tbsp/15–30 ml (½–1 fl oz) olive oil
1 onion, chopped
2 cloves garlic, chopped
425 g (15 oz) can tomatoes
1 tbsp/15 ml (½ fl oz) tomato paste
2 tsp dried oregano
salt and freshly ground black pepper

1 Preheat the oven to 200°C/400°F/Gas Mark 6.
   Roll out the pastry and line eight greased fluted
   tartlet tins. Prick with a fork and pre-bake for 20
   minutes until golden. Remove tartlet crusts from
   the oven and turn the heat down to 180°C/350°F/
   Gas Mark 4.
2 In the meantime, make the tomato sauce. Heat
   the oil in a saucepan and add the onion and
   garlic. Cook until soft. Add the tomatoes, tomato
   paste, oregano and seasoning. Simmer for
   5 minutes, then blend in a blender and keep hot.
3 Cook the peas until mushy, then drain and purée
   them in a blender. Heat the butter in a saucepan
   and stir in the pea purée. Season well with salt
   and plenty of black pepper. Divide the pea purée
   among the tart cases.
4 Poach the eggs until just set. Lift them carefully
   into the tart crusts and return to the oven for
   2–3 minutes. Don't let the eggs harden. Serve
   each tart with a spoonful of tomato sauce.

Spinach Roulade

Serves 6–8

700 g (1½ lb) fresh spinach, washed and
    picked over
1 tbsp butter
4 eggs, separated
grated nutmeg
salt and freshly ground black pepper
100 g (4 oz) cottage cheese
150 ml (¼ pt) sour cream
4 scallions, finely chopped

1 Cook the spinach without any additional water.
   Drain the spinach very well (press it between
   two plates for most the effective drainage) and
   when all the liquid has been removed, either chop
   it very finely or blend it just enough to chop it.
2 Add the butter, egg yolks, grated nutmeg and salt
   and pepper to taste. Mix together very well.
3 Whisk the egg whites until they are stiff. Fold a
   spoonful of the beaten whites into the spinach
   mixture to lighten it and then fold in the remaining
   whites. Mix through carefully.
4 Pour the mixture into a jelly roll tin 28 x 25 cm
   (15 x 10 in) that has been lined with parchment
   paper or foil. Bake at 200°C/400°F/Gas Mark 6 for
   10 minutes only.
5 While the spinach is cooking, mix the cottage
   cheese with the sour cream and scallion. Season
   to taste. Have a clean towel spread on a board
   and, when the spinach mixture is cooked, turn
   it upside down onto the towel. Carefully peel off
   the paper. Spread the cheese and sour cream
   mixture over the spinach base, taking care not to
   tear the surface. Using the towel to help you roll
   the spinach up into a roll and onto a serving plate.
   Serve immediately.

Nut Loaf

Serves 4

175 g (6 oz) mixed nuts, chopped
1 small eggplant
salt and freshly ground black pepper
olive oil
1 large onion, finely chopped
2 cloves garlic, chopped
175 g (6 oz) brown rice, cooked
200 g (7 oz) canned tomatoes, mashed
2 eggs, beaten

1 Preheat the oven to 190°C/375°F/Gas Mark 5. Put
   the nuts on a baking sheet and toast them at the
   top of the oven for 10 minutes.
2 Slice the eggplant, sprinkle with salt and leave for
   20 minutes. Rinse off the salt, pat dry and dice.
3 Heat 1–2 tbsp oil in a saucepan. Add the onion
   and garlic and fry until translucent. Add the
   eggplant and cook, stirring occasionally, for about
   10 minutes. Add more oil as necessary.
4 Transfer the eggplant mixture to a large bowl and
   stir in the nuts, brown rice and tomatoes. Mix well
   and season to taste. Stir in the beaten egg.
5 Pour into a small greased loaf tin and smooth the
   top. Bake in the center of the oven for 35 minutes
   until firm. Turn out of the pan and cut into slices
   to serve.

Mushroom and Broccoli Nut Loaf

Serves 6

50 g (2 oz) sliced button mushrooms

2 tbsp polyunsaturated margarine

2 stalks celery, chopped

1 clove garlic, crushed

1 onion, grated

1 tbsp whole wheat flour

400 g (15 oz) canned chopped tomatoes

100 g (4 oz) whole wheat breadcrumbs

100 g (4 oz) ground walnuts

1 egg

1 tsp fresh basil, chopped

1 tsp fresh oregano, chopped

1 tbsp parsley, chopped

salt and freshly ground black pepper

100 g (4 oz) broccoli spears, cooked

Sauce

50 g (2 oz) chopped mushrooms

3 tbsp whole wheat flour

120 ml (4 fl oz) vegetable stock

120 ml (4 fl oz) skim milk

celery leaves

1 Sauté the mushroom slices in a frying pan with 1 tbsp margarine, drain and place in a line down the center of a lightly greased 1.1 l (2 pt) loaf pan. Cook the celery, garlic and onion in the saucepan until softened. Mix in the flour and tomatoes and stir until thickened.

2 Add the breadcrumbs, nuts, egg, herbs and seasoning. Place half in the tin. Add the broccoli spears and top with the remaining mixture.

3 Cover with foil, place in a roasting tin filled with boiling water and cook at 180°C/350°F/Gas Mark 4 for 1¼–1½ hours.

4 Melt the remaining margarine, add the chopped mushrooms and cook for 2–3 minutes. Stir in the flour, and cook for 1 minute.

5 Add the stock, milk and seasoning and stir until boiled.

6 Turn out the loaf, garnish with celery leaves and serve the sauce separately.

Summer Vegetable Pasties

Makes 4

1 recipe Wholewheat Pastry (page 147)

beaten egg to glaze

Filling

100 g (4 oz) potatoes, diced

4 baby carrots, sliced

50 g (2 oz) peas

2 baby zucchini, sliced

2 stalks celery, sliced

½ green pepper, diced

Cheese sauce

2 tbsp butter

4 tbsp plain flour

300 ml (10 fl oz) milk

50 g (2 oz) Cheddar cheese, grated

salt

freshly ground black pepper

1 Make the pastry. Preheat the oven to 180°C/350°F/Gas Mark 4.

2 Boil the potatoes and carrots in salted water until just tender. In another saucepan, boil the remaining vegetables for about 2 minutes. Drain.

3 To make the cheese sauce, melt the butter in a heavy-bottomed saucepan, stir in the flour and gradually add half the milk, stirring. Add the cheese. Stir until melted. Add a little more milk and season to taste. Don't make the sauce too thin or it will pour out of the pastry shells. Mix the sauce into the vegetables to coat them generously.

4 Divide the pastry into 4 balls and roll out. Share the mixture between the pastry rounds. Crimp together to form pasties and brush with beaten egg. Put the pasties on a baking tray and bake in the oven for 30 minutes or until the pastry is cooked.

Sabzi Vegetable Cutlet

Serves 4–6
100 g (4 oz) beet, grated
100 g (4 oz) carrots, grated
225 g (8 oz) potatoes, grated
100 g (4 oz) cabbage, shredded
½ tsp chili powder
½ tsp ground roasted cumin
salt and freshly ground black pepper
large pinch sugar
1 tbsp raisins (optional)
50 g (2 oz) flour
120 ml (4 oz) milk
oil for deep frying

1 Mix the vegetables with the chili, roasted cumin, black pepper, salt, sugar and raisins. Divide into 12 balls and flatten. Chill for 1 hour.
2 Make a batter with the flour and milk and dip a cutlet in it.
3 Heat the oil in a large frying pan and fry the cutlets for 2–3 minutes, turning once, until crisp and golden. Serve with cilantro chutney (see page 123).

Spinach Ring

Serves 4
900 g (2 lb) spinach
6 tbsp butter
salt and freshly ground
    black pepper
50 g (2 oz) unbleached
    plain flour
300 ml (10 fl oz) milk
50 g (2 oz) Parmesan
    cheese
3 eggs

Tomato sauce
1–2 tbsp) oil
1 onion, finely chopped
2 cloves garlic,
    crushed
425 g (15 oz) canned
    tomatoes, mashed
1 tbsp tomato paste

1   Preheat the oven to 190°C/375°F/Gas Mark
    5. Grease a 1.7 l (3 pt) ring mold.
2   Wash the spinach and discard any tough stalks.
    Pack spinach into a large saucepan with 2 tbsp
    butter and seasoning and cover tightly. Cook over
    low heat for about 5 minutes, stirring occasionally,
    until spinach is soft. Drain and purée in a blender.
3   Now make the cheese sauce. Melt the rest of the
    butter in a heavy-bottomed saucepan and add
    the flour, stirring. Gradually add the milk, stirring
    continuously. Stir in the cheese and season. Stir
    until the sauce bubbles and thickens, then turn
    down the heat and cook for one more minute. Mix
    thoroughly with the spinach.
4   Separate the eggs. Beat the yolks into the spinach
    mixture. Whisk the whites until soft peaks have
    formed and fold into mixture. Pour mixture into
    ring mold and bake for 30–40 minutes until risen
    and lightly set.
5   Meanwhile, make the tomato sauce. Heat the
    oil in a frying pan and add the onion and garlic.
    Fry, stirring, until transparent. Add the tomatoes,
    reserving the juice. Add the tomato paste
    and season. Simmer for 5 minutes, adding more
    juice and adjusting seasoning as necessary.
6   To turn out the spinach ring, dip mold into ice-cold
    water for a few seconds. Run a knife blade around
    the edges of the mold. Invert onto a warmed plate.
    Spoon over the tomato sauce and serve with
    wholewheat bread.

Chinese Eight Treasures

Serves 4–6
15 g (½ oz) dried tiger lily buds
3–4 tbsp/15 g (½ oz) dried wood ear mushrooms
10 g (⅓ oz) dried black moss
225 (8 oz) tofu
50 g (2 oz) bamboo shoots
50 g (2 oz) lotus root
50 g (2 oz) straw mushrooms
50 g (2 oz) cashew nuts or almonds
4 tbsp oil
1½ tsp salt
1 tsp sugar
1 tbsp light soy sauce
1 tsp cornstarch mixed with 1 tbsp cold water
2 tsp sesame oil

1   Soak the dried vegetables separately in cold water
    overnight or in warm water for at least 1 hour. Cut
    the tofu into short lengths.
2   Cut the bamboo shoots and lotus root into small
    slices. The straw mushrooms and white nuts can
    be left whole.
3   Heat a wok or large frying pan. When it is hot, put
    in about half of the oil and wait until it smokes.
    Stirfry all the dried vegetables together with a little
    salt for about 1 minute. Remove and set aside.
4   Add and heat the remaining oil and stirfry the rest
    of the vegetables and the remaining salt for about
    1 minute. Add the partly cooked dried vegetables,
    the sugar and soy sauce, stirring constantly.
    If the contents start to dry out, pour in a little
    water. When the vegetables are cooked, add the
    cornstarch and water mixture to thicken the sauce.
    Garnish with the sesame oil just before serving.
    This dish can be served hot or cold.

Stirfried Mixed Vegetables

Serves 4

5–6 dried Chinese mushrooms
100 g (4 oz) snow peas
100 g (4 oz) Chinese cabbage
100 g (4 oz) carrots
1 red chili
3 tbsp oil
1 tsp salt
1 tsp sugar
1 tsp water

1   Soak the dried mushrooms in warm water for 25–30 minutes. Squeeze them dry, discard the hard stalks and cut into thin slices. Trim the snow peas and cut the Chinese cabbage and carrots into slices.

2   Heat the oil in a preheated wok. Add the Chinese cabbage, carrots, snow peas, chili and dried mushroom and stirfry for about 1 minute. Add the salt and sugar and stir for another minute or so with a little more water if necessary. Do not overcook or the vegetables will lose their crunchiness. Serve hot with buckwheat noodles.

Chinese Three Precious Jewels

Serves 4

225 (8 oz) tofu
225 g (8 oz) broccoli or snow peas
225 g (8 oz) carrots
4 tbsp oil
1 tsp salt
1 tsp sugar
1 tbsp rice wine or dry sherry
1 tbsp light soy sauce

1   Cut the tofu into small pieces. Cut the broccoli into florets. Cut the snow peas diagonally into small pieces. Peel the carrots and cut diagonally into small chunks.

2   Heat about half of the oil in a hot wok or frying pan. Add the tofu pieces and shallow fry on both sides until golden. Remove and set aside.

3   Heat the rest of the oil. When very hot, stirfry the broccoli and carrots for about 1–1½ minutes. Add the tofu, salt, sugar, wine and soy sauce and continue stirring, adding a little water if necessary. Cook for 2–3 minutes if you like the broccoli and carrots to be crunchy. If not, cook another minute or two. This dish is best served hot.

Curried Vegetables

Serves 4
225 g (8 oz) eggplant, cut into chunks
2 tbsp oil
50 g (2 oz) cashew nuts
1 medium onion, chopped
1 clove garlic, crushed
2 tsp curry powder
1 large potato, peeled and half-cooked
100 g (4 oz) green beans, trimmed
150 ml (¼ pt) water
100 g (4 oz) tomatoes, quartered
1 tbsp garam masala
150 ml (¼ pt) yogurt
2 tsp cornstarch
1 tbsp water
salt

1 Salt the eggplant and leave for 30 minutes.
2 Rinse and pat dry.
3 Heat the oil and fry the cashews to a golden brown. Remove them from the saucepan and put them aside.
4 Stir the onions and garlic into the saucepan and cook until they begin to soften. Add the curry powder and stir in. Add the eggplant and cook on low heat for about 5 minutes, stirring from time to time. Add a little more oil if necessary.
5 Add the half-cooked potato, cut into large chunks, and the green beans. Pour on the water, cover and leave to cook until the potatoes are ready.
6 Add the tomatoes and the garam masala, stir carefully and continue cooking for a few more minutes.
7 Mix the cornstarch with the water into a smooth paste, stir into the contents of the saucepan and warm through for 3 minutes.
8 Serve hot, with the browned cashew nuts sprinkled on top.

Chinese Mixed Vegetable Casserole

Serves 4–6
2 tbsp/10 g (⅓ oz) dried wood ear mushrooms
225 (8 oz) tofu
100 g (4 oz) green beans or snow peas
100 g (4 oz) cabbage or broccoli
100 g (4 oz) baby corn or bamboo shoots
100 g (4 oz) carrots
3–4 tbsp oil
1 tsp salt
1 tsp sugar
1 tbsp light soy sauce
1 tsp cornstarch mixed with 1 tbsp cold water

1 Soak the wood ear mushrooms in water for 20–25 minutes, rinse and discard the hard roots.
2 Cut the tofu into about 12 small pieces and harden the pieces in a pot of lightly salted boiling water for 2–3 minutes. Remove and drain.
3 Trim the green beans or snow peas. Cut the vegetables into thin slices or chunks.
4 Heat about half of the oil in a flameproof casserole or saucepan. When hot, lightly brown the tofu on both sides. Remove with a slotted spoon and set aside.
5 Heat the remaining oil and stirfry the rest of the vegetables for about 1½ minutes. Add the tofu pieces, salt, sugar and soy sauce and continue stirring to blend everything well. Cover, reduce the heat and simmer for 2–3 minutes.
6 Mix the cornstarch with water to make a smooth paste, pour it over the vegetables and stir. Increase the heat to high just long enough to thicken the sauce. Serve hot.

Sichuan Tofu Casserole

Serves 4

2 tbsp dried wood ear mushrooms or dried
   Chinese mushrooms
225 g (8 oz) tofu
1–2 leeks or 2–3 scallions
3 tbsp oil
1 tsp salted black beans
1 tbsp chili paste
2 tbsp rice wine or dry sherry
1 tbsp light soy sauce
1 tsp cornstarch mixed with 1 tbsp cold water
Sichuan pepper, freshly ground

1 Soak the wood ear mushrooms in water for 20–25 minutes, rinse them clean, discard any hard roots and then drain. If you use dried mushrooms, they should be soaked in hot or warm water for at least 30–35 minutes. Squeeze them dry, throw out the hard stalks and cut into small pieces, retaining the water for later use.

2 Cut the tofu into 1 cm (½ in) cubes. Blanch in a saucepan of boiling water for 2–3 minutes, remove and drain. Cut the leeks or scallions into short lengths.

3 Heat the oil in a hot wok until it smokes and stirfry the leeks or scallions and the wood ear mushrooms or mushrooms for about 1 minute. Add the salted black beans, crush them with a spatula and blend well.

4 Now add the tofu, the chili bean paste, rice wine or sherry and soy sauce and continue stirring to blend. Add a little water and cook for 3–4 more minutes. Finally, add the cornstarch and water mixture to thicken the sauce. Serve hot with freshly ground Sichuan pepper to garnish.

Vegetable Chop Suey

Serves 4–6

225 g (8 oz) tofu
2 tbsp wood ear mushrooms, dried
175 g (6 oz) broccoli or snow peas
175 g (6 oz) bamboo shoots
4–5 tbsp oil
1½ tsp salt
1 tsp sugar
1–2 scallions, finely chopped
1 tbsp light soy sauce
2 tbsp rice wine or dry sherry
1 tsp cornstarch mixed with 1 tbsp cold water

1 Cut the tofu into about 24 small pieces. Soak the wood ear mushrooms in water for about 20–25 minutes, rinse them clean and discard any hard roots. Cut the broccoli and bamboo shoots into uniformly small pieces.

2 Heat a wok over a high heat, add about half of the oil and wait for it to smoke. Swirl the wok so that its surface is well greased. Add the tofu pieces and shallow fry them on both sides until golden, then scoop out with a slotted spoon and set them aside.

3 Heat the remaining oil and add the broccoli. Stir for about 30 seconds and then add the wood ear mushrooms, bamboo shoots and the partly cooked tofu. Continue stirring for 1 minute and then add the salt, sugar, scallions, soy sauce and wine. Blend well and, when the sauce starts to boil, thicken it with the cornstarch and water mixture. Serve hot.

Bean Moussaka

Serves 4

225 g (8 oz) kidney
    beans
1 large eggplant, thinly
    sliced
salt and freshly ground
    black pepper
oil
1 large onion, chopped
2 cloves garlic,
    chopped
400 g (15 oz) canned
    tomatoes, mashed

1 tbsp tomato paste
2 tsp fresh thyme,
    chopped

Cheese sauce

2 tbsp butter
4 tbsp flour
300 ml (10 fl oz) milk
50 g (2 oz) grated
    Cheddar cheese
grated nutmeg to taste

1   Soak the beans overnight and cook until you can
    mash them with a fork. Drain.

2   Heat the oven to 350°F/180°C/Gas Mark 4.
    Sprinkle the eggplant slices with salt and allow
    to stand in a colander for 30 minutes. Rinse
    and pat dry with paper towels. Heat some oil in
    a saucepan and fry the eggplants gently until
    cooked. Set aside.

3   Add some more oil to the saucepan and fry
    the onion and garlic until translucent. Add the
    tomatoes, tomato paste, thyme and seasoning,
    and heat through, stirring. Mix in the beans.

4   To make the cheese sauce, melt the butter in a
    thick-bottomed saucepan. Stir in the flour, then
    gradually add the milk, stirring all the time, until
    the sauce bubbles and thickens. Turn down the
    heat, add the cheese and stir until melted. Season
    with nutmeg and add salt and pepper to taste.

5   To assemble the dish, spread a layer of the
    bean mixture in the bottom of a casserole dish
    and top with eggplant slices. Spread thinly with
    cheese sauce. Continue to layer the ingredients,
    ending with a thick layer of the sauce. Bake in the
    oven for 30–40 minutes and serve with a crisp
    green salad.

Vegetable Couscous

Serves 4–6
100–175 g (4–6 oz) couscous
1 tsp salt
300 ml (10 fl oz) boiling water
3 tbsp/40 g (1½ oz) butter

Vegetable topping
1 tbsp/15 ml (½ fl oz) oil
2 large onions, chopped
2 leeks, sliced
4 carrots, sliced
1 l (2 pts) stock
salt and freshly ground black pepper
4 zucchini, sliced
6 tomatoes, sliced
100 g (4 oz) peas
100 g (4 oz) kidney beans, pre-soaked
   and cooked
100 g (4 oz) chickpeas, pre-soaked and cooked
a few strands of saffron

1 Put the couscous in a bowl, add the salt and pour over the boiling water. Let it soak for 20 minutes until the water has been absorbed. Break up any lumps that are sticking together.

2 Meanwhile, make the vegetable topping. Heat the oil in a large saucepan and stirfry the onions and leeks. Add the carrots and stock and season well. Bring to a boil.

3 Place the couscous in a vegetable steamer (or a sift or colander) lined with muslin, and put this over the saucepan. Put on the lid and simmer for 30 minutes.

4 Remove the steamer and add the remaining vegetables and the saffron to the stock. Stir the couscous with a fork to break up any lumps. Replace steamer, covered, and continue cooking for 10 minutes.

5 Put the couscous into a bowl and stir in the butter. Serve vegetables separately and offer Hot Tomato Sauce and pita bread (see pages 116 and 141).

Bulgur Wheat Stuffed Peppers

Serves 4

150 g (5 oz) bulgur wheat
2 red peppers, cut in half lengthways
   and seeded
2 yellow peppers, cut in half lengthways
   and seeded
1 tbsp sunflower oil
1 onion, chopped
50 g (2 oz) chopped hazelnuts
75 g (3 oz) chopped dried apricots
½ tsp powdered ginger
l tsp cardamom seeds, ground
3 tbsp plain yogurt
fresh cilantro leaves

1 Place the bulgur wheat in a bowl, pour over 300 ml (10 fl oz) boiling water and leave to stand for 15 minutes. Place the peppers in a shallow, lightly oiled ovenproof dish.
2 Place the remaining oil in a saucepan, add the onion and gently fry until softened.
3 Stir in the bulgur wheat, hazelnuts, apricots, ginger and cardamom. Cook for 1 minute, stirring continuously.
4 Add chopped cilantro and yogurt, mix together and use to fill the pepper shells. Cover the dish tightly with aluminium foil and bake in a preheated oven at 190°C/375°F/Gas Mark 5 for 30–35 minutes.
5 Serve immediately, garnished with cilantro leaves.

Paprika Mushrooms

Serves 4

butter or margarine
1 medium onion, finely chopped
½ green pepper, finely chopped
1 tbsp paprika
350 g (12 oz) mushrooms, sliced
150 ml (¼ pt) sour cream
salt and freshly ground black pepper
chopped parsley

1 Heat the butter, add the onion and cook until it has just softened but not browned.
2 Add the green pepper and paprika and cook on low heat for 3 minutes. Add the mushrooms, stir well and cook for 5 more minutes until they are soft.
3 Stir in the sour cream, season to taste and warm through gently.
4 Serve, sprinkled with parsley.

Savory Stuffed Grape Leaves

Serves 4

225 g (8 oz) brown rice
olive oil
1 small onion, chopped
2 cloves garlic, chopped
225 g (8 oz) peeled bottled or canned chestnuts
1–2 tbsp butter
100 g (4 oz) mushrooms
2 tomatoes, peeled and chopped
l tsp dried mixed herbs
salt and freshly ground black pepper
20 grape leaves

1 Wash the rice in several changes of cold water. Heat 1 tbsp oil in a heavy-bottomed saucepan and fry the onion and garlic until translucent. Stir in the rice and cook for a few minutes before covering with boiling water. (Use about ⅔ water to ⅓ rice by volume). Bring back to a boil, then cover the saucepan and turn the heat down very low. The rice should be cooked in about 40 minutes.

2 Meanwhile, drain the chestnuts and chop them finely. Heat the butter in a saucepan and add the mushrooms. When they are tender, add the tomatoes, chestnuts and herbs. Stir once or twice and remove from the heat.

3 When the rice is cooked, mix it thoroughly with the nut stuffing and check the seasoning. Use it, by the spoonful, to stuff the grape leaves. Pack them into an ovenproof dish, brush with olive oil and cover the dish with foil. Heat through in the oven. Stuffed grape leaves are best eaten hot, but they're good cold too, if you have any left over.

4 Serve with lemon slices.

Mushroom Omelet Surprise

Serves 2

100 g (4 oz) mushrooms
150 ml (5 fl oz) milk
1 tbsp butter
1 tbsp flour
1 tbsp grated Parmesan cheese
salt and freshly ground black pepper
4 eggs, separated

1 Peel or wipe the mushrooms and slice. Put them in a small, heavy-bottomed saucepan with a little of the milk and poach gently until very black and juicy. Remove the mushrooms with a slotted spoon and arrange them in the bottom of a shallow greased heatproof dish about 18 cm (7 in) in diameter.

2 Make a cheese sauce. Heat the butter in a saucepan and when it has melted, add the flour. Stir well and remove from the heat. Add the milk that the mushrooms have been cooked in and stir in enough extra milk to make a thick sauce. Stir in the cheese and season well.

3 Beat the yolks into the cheese sauce. Whisk the whites until they form soft peaks and fold into the sauce.

4 Pour the mixture over the mushrooms and cook under a preheated grill until the omelet is nearly set and golden on top.

Potato-topped Vegetable Pie

Serves 4–6

75 g (3 oz) green lentils
50 g (2 oz) pearl barley
1 onion, peeled and chopped
400 ml (15 oz) canned chopped tomatoes
175 g (6 oz) cauliflower florets
2 stalks celery, sliced
1 leek, thickly sliced
1 turnip, peeled and sliced
2 carrots, peeled and diced
2 tbsp fresh mixed herbs, chopped
750 g (1½ lb) potatoes, scrubbed
3 tbsp 2% milk
salt
freshly ground black pepper
2 tbsp medium hard cheese, grated

1 Place the lentils, barley, onion, tomatoes, cauliflower, celery, leek, turnip, carrots and herbs in a large saucepan with 300 ml (10 fl oz) water.

2 Bring to a boil, cover and simmer for 40–45 minutes or until everything is soft.

3 Cover potatoes with boiling water and cook for about 15 minutes, or until soft.

4 Drain, peel and mash the potatoes with the milk and season to taste.

5 Place the lentils mix in a pie dish and either pipe or fork the potato on top.

6 Sprinkle with cheese and cook in a preheated oven at 200°C/400°F/Gas Mark 6 for 30–35 minutes.

Cheesy Mushroom Omelet

Serves 2
2 tbsp butter
4 tbsp flour
150 ml (5 fl oz) milk
40 g (1½ oz) grated Cheddar cheese
3 eggs
salt and freshly ground black pepper
a handful of button or chestnut
    mushrooms, sliced

1 Melt the butter in a saucepan and stir in the flour. Gradually stir in the milk until you have a smooth sauce. Add the cheese and stir until melted.
2 Beat the eggs and season well.
3 Put the mushrooms in a shallow ovenproof dish about 22 cm (8 in) across. Cover with cheese sauce, then pour over the beaten eggs. Broil for about 7 minutes until the egg is nearly set and the omelet is beginning to brown on top.
4 Serve with salad.

Fried "Pocketed Eggs"

Serves 4
2–3 tbsp oil
4 eggs
1 tbsp/15 ml (½ fl oz) light soy sauce
1 scallion, finely chopped

1 Heat the oil in a hot wok or frying pan and fry the eggs on both sides. Add the soy sauce and a little water and braise for 1–2 minutes. Garnish with scallions and serve hot.

Cook's Tip
Taking a bite of the egg and finding the yolk inside the white is rather like finding something in a pocket—hence the name of this dish.

Avocado Soufflé Omelet

Serves 2
1 green pepper
3 tbsp butter
1 ripe avocado
dash lemon juice
4 eggs, separated
salt and freshly ground black pepper

1 De-seed and slice the green pepper. Heat a little of the butter in a saucepan and fry gently until soft. Set aside.

2 Cut the avocado in half. Remove the stone and remove the flesh from the shell in one careful movement with a palette knife. Slice the avocado and sprinkle with lemon juice.

3 Beat the egg yolks and season with salt and pepper. Whisk the whites and fold the two together.

4 Heat half of the remaining butter in a saucepan and pour in half the omelet mixture. Arrange half the avocado and green pepper on one side of it. When lightly set, fold the omelet in half, slide it out of the saucepan and keep it hot until you have made the second omelet in the same way.

Fu Yung Tofu

Serves 4
225 g (8 oz) tofu
1 tsp salt
4 egg whites
1 tbsp cornstarch mixed with 2 tbsp water
60 ml (2 fl oz) milk
1 romaine lettuce heart
50 g (2 oz) green peas
oil for deep frying
1 scallion, finely chopped
½ tsp fresh ginger, grated
1 tsp sesame oil

1 Cut the tofu into long, thin strips and blanch in a saucepan of salted boiling water to harden. Remove and drain.

2 Lightly beat the egg whites. Add the cornstarch mixture and milk.

3 Wash and separate the lettuce heart. If you use frozen peas, make sure they are thoroughly defrosted.

4 Wait for the tofu to cook and then coat with the egg whites, cornstarch and milk mixture.

5 Heat the oil in a wok or deep fryer until it is very hot. Turn off the heat and let the oil cool a bit before adding the tofu coated with the egg whites and cornstarch mixture. Cook for about 1–1½ minutes and then scoop out with a slotted spoon and drain.

6 Pour off the excess oil, leaving about 1 tbsp in the wok. Increase the heat and stirfry the lettuce heart with a pinch of salt. Remove and set aside on a serving dish.

7 Heat another tbsp of oil in the wok and add the finely chopped scallion and ginger followed by the peas, salt and a little water. When the mixture starts to boil, add the tofu strips. Blend well, add the sesame oil, and serve on the lettuce heart.

Leek and Stilton Bake

Serves 4

450 g (1 lb) small leeks
6 eggs
2 tbsp cider vinegar
1 slice white bread, made into breadcrumbs
100 g (4 oz) Stilton cheese

1 Pre-heat the oven to 200°C/400°F/Gas Mark 6. Trim and wash the leeks. Steam for 10–15 minutes and lay them in a greased ovenproof dish.

2 Beat the eggs with the vinegar and crumble in the Stilton. Pour over the leeks and top with the breadcrumbs.

3 Bake in the oven for 30 minutes until golden and the breadcrumbs have formed a crust on the top.

Broccoli and Tomato Cheesecake

Serves 4–6
100 g (4 oz) wholewheat cracker crumbs
4 tbsp butter, softened

Filling
250 g (8 oz) broccoli florets
salt and freshly ground white pepper
1 large tomato
350 g (12 oz) cottage cheese
pinch nutmeg
2 eggs, separated

Topping
broccoli florets, cooked

1 Pre-heat the oven to 350°F/180°C/Gas Mark 4. Combine the crumbs and the butter and press down well into a greased 22 cm (8 in) springform pan.
2 Steam the broccoli florets over boiling salted water until tender. Carefully slice some of the florets for decorating and reserve the rest. Immerse the tomato in boiling water for a minute, refresh in cold water, peel and de-seed.
3 Mash the cottage cheese with the broccoli and tomato and season well with salt, pepper and a good pinch of nutmeg. Beat in the egg yolks.
4 Whisk the whites until they form soft peaks and fold into the mixture. Pour the filling over the crumb base and bake for about 20–25 minutes until slightly risen and just set.
5 Leave to cool. When cold, remove the sides of the tin and decorate the top with the remaining broccoli florets.

Chinese Scrambled Eggs and Tomatoes

Serves 4
250 g (9 oz) tomatoes
5 eggs
1½ tsp salt
2 scallions, finely chopped
1 tsp fresh ginger, finely chopped (optional)
4 tbsp oil

1 Scald the tomatoes in a bowl of boiling water and peel off the skins. Cut each tomato in half lengthways and then cut each half into wedges.
2 Beat the eggs with a pinch of salt and about a third of the finely chopped scallions.
3 Heat about half of the oil in a hot wok or frying pan and lightly scramble the eggs over moderate heat until set. Remove the eggs from the wok.
4 Heat the wok again over high heat and add the remaining oil. When the oil is hot, add the rest of the finely chopped scallions, the fresh ginger (if used) and the tomatoes. Stir a few times and then add the scrambled eggs with the remaining salt. Stir for 1 minute more and serve hot.

Cook's Tip
Other vegetables such as cucumber, green peppers or green peas can be substituted for the tomatoes.

Savory Cheesecake

Serves 4–6
ready made pie crust (enough for a 20 cm/8 in pie) or a crumb base
butter
1 large onion, sliced
4 eggs
225 g (8 oz) cottage cheese
225 g (8 oz) cream cheese
chopped chives
salt and freshly ground black pepper

1 Put the pastry case into a springform pan. Heat the butter, add the onion and cook until it has just softened but not browned.

2 Beat the eggs until they are very light and fluffy. Mix the cheeses with the cooked onion, chives, salt and pepper. Carefully fold the cheese mixture into the beaten eggs and spoon this into the prepared pastry case.

3 Bake at 350°F/180°C/Gas Mark 4 for 40 minutes.

4 Serve cold (preferably the next day) with a crisp salad. This freezes very well. Leeks make a tasty addition with the onions, softened in a little butter.

Vegetable and Rice Hotch Potch

Serves 6

oil
350 g (12 oz) onions, sliced
225 g (8 oz) rice
1 large green or red pepper, chopped
salt and freshly ground black pepper
1 tsp paprika
400 g (15 oz) can of tomatoes
150 ml (5 fl oz) water
600 ml (1 pt) yogurt
4 eggs

1 Heat the oil, add the onions and cook until they have just softened but not browned.
2 Add the rice and peppers and stir to color them a little. Season well with salt, pepper and paprika.
3 Layer the rice mixture with the tomatoes in an ovenproof dish. Pour over a mixture of 4 tbsp oil and the water.
4 Cover and cook at 190°C/375°F/Gas Mark 5 for 30 minutes (or a medium heat).
5 Mix the yogurt with the eggs. Pour over the vegetables and return the dish, uncovered, to the oven for 20 more minutes.

Variation

This Bulgarian dish adapts to endless variations— add some more vegetables, such as eggplants, zucchini, mushrooms, fennel.

Cheese Strudel

Serves 4

350 g (12 oz) packet puff pastry
175 g (6 oz) grated Cheddar cheese
100 g (4 oz) cream cheese
100 g (4 oz) cottage cheese
1 egg, separated
chopped parsley or mint
salt and freshly ground black pepper
egg white for glazing

1 Roll the pastry out as thinly as possible.
2 Mix the remaining ingredients, except the egg white, until smooth. Spread the mixture over the pastry.
3 Fold over to make a flattish strip, sealing the edges well. Brush with the egg white. Place on a moistened baking sheet and bake at 200°C/400°F/Gas Mark 6 for 20 minutes.
4 Serve hot, with sour cream.

VEGETABLE AND RICE SIDE DISHES

There are some dishes that satisfy as main courses and others that serve best as complements to them. They round out our enjoyment of a meal and fulfill nutritional requirements. Potatoes, rice and bean recipes, and a wide selection of green and root vegetables take to the table in Continental, Indian and Oriental styles.

Zucchini Gratin

Serves 4

oil
4 large/450 g (1 lb) zucchini, sliced
1 large onion, chopped
400 g (15 oz) canned tomatoes
chopped basil, thyme or marjoram
sliver lemon peel
salt and freshly ground black pepper
225 g (8 oz) macaroni
2 eggs
150 ml (5 fl oz) yogurt
75 g (2½ oz) grated Cheddar cheese

1 Heat the oil and fry the zucchini until they are lightly colored. Remove them from the saucepan and reserve. Add the onion and fry until golden, adding more oil if necessary. Add the tomatoes, herbs, lemon peel, salt and pepper and simmer for 10 minutes, breaking up the tomatoes and stirring from time to time.
2 Meanwhile, cook the macaroni and drain it well. Put it into an ovenproof dish.
3 Pour the sauce over the macaroni and mix well. Lay the cooked zucchini on top. Mix the eggs, yogurt and half of the cheese and pour the mixture over the zucchini. Scatter the remaining cheese on top.
4 Bake the dish at 190°C/375°F/Gas Mark 5 for 30 minutes.

Variation

You could use eggplants instead of zucchini, in which case slice and salt them, leave them to drain for 20 minutes, rinse and dry them and proceed as above.

Zucchini with Almonds

Serves 4

6 large/700 g (1½ lb) zucchini, sliced lengthways
1 medium onion, finely chopped
1 tbsp olive oil
salt and freshly ground black pepper
50 g (2 oz) flaked almonds
1 tsp cornstarch
1 tbsp water
250 ml (8 fl oz) yogurt

1 Place the zucchini in a shallow ovenproof dish. Mix the onion, oil, salt and pepper and spoon the mixture over the zucchini. Bake uncovered at 180°C/350°F/Gas Mark 4 for 40 minutes, or until tender.
2 Meanwhile toast the almonds: put them into a heavy frying pan over high heat and shake the pan frequently; don't burn.
3 Mix the cornstarch with the water and add it to the yogurt with seasoning to taste.
4 Warm the mixture over a gentle heat, stirring constantly, for 3 minutes.
5 Spoon it over the zucchini and scatter the almonds on top.

Zucchini with Dill

Serves 4

60 ml (2 fl oz) olive oil

2 tbsp butter

1 onion, chopped

1 garlic, crushed

450 g (1 lb) zucchini
topped, tailed
and sliced in
thickish rounds

salt and freshly ground
black pepper

2 tsp paprika

1 tbsp dill, chopped
(not the stalks)

1 small tub sour cream

1   Heat oil and butter in a large frying pan. Cook the onion and garlic gently until soft. Turn up the heat.

2   Add the zucchini and black pepper and toss. Cook for 5–10 minutes, stirring to cook both sides of the zucchini slices. When browning, add the paprika, dill and sour cream. Season and serve.

Magyar Marrow or Squash

Serves 4

1 medium to large marrow (summer squash)

2 tbsp butter

2 tsp cornstarch

1 tbsp water

1 tbsp dried dill

salt and freshly ground black pepper

150 ml (5 fl oz) sour cream

1   Peel the marrow and either finely chop or grate it. Cook the marrow with the butter, stirring from time to time, just until it begins to soften. Mix the cornstarch with the water until smooth and add it to the marrow. Stir and cook for 3 more minutes

2   Add the dill, salt and pepper and finally stir in the sour cream. Warm it through gently and serve the marrow hot.

Chili Beans

Serves 4

175 g (6 oz) tinned kidney beans

2 tbsp olive oil

½ tsp fennel seeds

½ tsp mustard seeds

1 onion, chopped

2 cloves garlic, chopped

100 g (4 oz) sliced mushrooms

½ fresh green chili, seeded and chopped

425 g (15 oz) canned tomatoes, mashed

2 tbsp, fresh cilantro or parsley, chopped

salt and freshly ground black pepper

1   Heat the oil in a saucepan and, when hot, add the seeds. As soon as the mustard seeds begin to pop, add the onion and garlic. Cook gently until translucent.

2   Stir in the mushrooms. When they are tender, add the chili and tomatoes, cilantro and seasoning.

3   Add the beans, heat through for 10 minutes and serve with cheese toast or an omelet for a warming winter supper.

Stuffed Marrow or Squash

Serves 4–6

1 marrow (summer squash)

salt and freshly ground black pepper

75 g (3 oz) brown rice

2 small carrots, diced

50 g (2 oz) peas

1–2 tbsp oil

1 onion, chopped

1 clove garlic, chopped

1 stalk celery, chopped

1 handful parsley, chopped

2 tbsp hazelnuts, chopped

Tomato sauce

1–2 tbsp oil

1 onion, chopped

2 cloves garlic, chopped

400 g (15 oz) canned tomatoes, mashed

1 tbsp tomato paste

salt and freshly ground black pepper

1 Preheat the oven to 180°C/350°F/Gas Mark 4. Cut the marrow in half lengthways and scoop out the pulp and seeds. Sprinkle the flesh with salt and leave the halves upside down to drain.

2 Meanwhile, make the filling. Simmer the rice in a covered saucepan of salted water until just tender (about 30 minutes). Drain.

3 Parboil carrots and peas and drain. Heat oil in a saucepan and fry the onion and garlic until translucent. Add celery, carrots and peas. Stir in the rice, parsley and hazelnuts and season well. Dry the marrow and pile the filling into one half of it. Top with the second half.

4 Make the tomato sauce. Heat oil in a saucepan and add onion and garlic. Fry, stirring, until soft. Add tomatoes and tomato paste. Simmer for 5 minutes, stirring occasionally, and season well.

5 Place marrow in a baking dish with a lid, or cover with foil. Surround it with the sauce. Cover and cook for 45 minutes until marrow is tender. Serve hot or cold with a crisp green salad.

Creamed Spinach

Serves 4

700 g (1½ lb) fresh spinach, washed and
    picked over
salt and freshly ground black pepper
1 egg yolk
grated nutmeg
150 ml (5 fl oz) yogurt

1 Cook the spinach (without adding any water) and a little salt. Drain the cooked spinach very well (press it between two plates for the most effective drainage).
2 Whisk together the egg yolk, nutmeg and seasoning to taste, and yogurt. Mix into the spinach. Warm through gently.

Cook's Tip
If you prefer to use frozen spinach, use whole-leaf, not chopped spinach.

La Lechuga

Serves 4

1 head crisp lettuce, such as iceberg
4 tbsp olive oil
4 cloves garlic, finely chopped

1 Discard the looser outer leaves of lettuce. With a very sharp knife, cut lettuce in half from stalk to tip. Cut each half into thirds. Keep cold.
2 Heat oil in frying pan and when hot, add garlic. Fry, stirring, until brown. Pour over the lettuce and serve immediately. This is best eaten with the fingers if you don't mind the mess. Offer plenty of paper napkins. Lettuce served this way makes an unusual and appetizing start to a summer meal.

Spicy Eggplant

Serves 4

450 g (1 lb) eggplants
3 tbsp oil
1 large onion, finely chopped
3 tomatoes, chopped
1 tbsp cilantro leaves, chopped
1–2 green chilis, chopped
½ tsp ground turmeric
½ tsp chili powder
¾ tsp ground cilantro ¾ tsp salt

1 Broil the eggplants for about 15 minutes, turning frequently until the skin turns black and the flesh soft. Peel off the skin and mash the flesh.
2 Heat the oil in a large saucepan over medium heat and fry the onion until soft. Add the tomatoes, cilantro leaves and green chilis and fry another 2–3 minutes.
3 Add the mashed eggplant, turmeric, chili, cilantro and salt and stir.
4 Fry for another 10–12 minutes and serve with Naan or Baktora Yogurt Bread (see page 144).

Cabbage with Peas

Serves 4

3 tbsp oil
2 bay leaves
¾ tsp whole
   cumin seeds
700 g (1½ lb) finely
   shredded cabbage
1 tsp ground turmeric
½ tsp chili powder

1½ tsp ground cumin
1 tsp ground cilantro
2 tomatoes, chopped
¾ tsp salt
½ tsp sugar
100 g (4 oz) peas

1 Heat the oil in a large saucepan over medium high heat and add the bay leaves and cumin seeds. Let them sizzle for a few seconds.
2 Add the cabbage and stir-fry for 2–3 minutes. Add the turmeric, chili, cumin, cilantro, tomatoes, salt and sugar and mix with the cabbage.
3 Lower the heat, cover and cook for 15 minutes. Add the peas and cover again. Continue to cook for 15 more minutes, stirring occasionally.
4 Remove the cover, turn heat up to medium high and, stirring continuously, cook until dry.

Brussels Sprouts with Garlic and Mushrooms

Serves 4

2–3 tbsp oil
4 cloves garlic, chopped
450 g (1 lb) Brussels sprouts, thinly sliced
100 g (4 oz) mushrooms, sliced

1 Heat some oil in a wok or deep-sided frying pan. Add the garlic and fry quickly, stirring, until crisp and brown.
2 Add the Brussels sprouts and mushrooms and stir until coated with garlic and oil. Stirfry for 1–2 minutes and eat while crisp and hot. This is a delicious accompaniment to bean dishes.

Caraway Cabbage

Serves 4

2 tbsp butter
700 g (1½ lb) finely sliced white or green cabbage
1 tbsp caraway seeds
salt and freshly ground black pepper
2 tsp flour
150 ml (5 fl oz) sour cream

1 Melt the butter in a large frying pan and add the cabbage. Stir well. Add the caraway seeds, salt and pepper, cover and cook until the cabbage is cooked but still crisp.
2 Add the flour and stir it in well. Cook for 2 more minutes, stirring constantly. Add the sour cream and warm it through.

Cauliflower with Potatoes and Peas

Serves 4–6
4 tbsp oil
2 medium onions, finely chopped
450 g (1 lb) diced potatoes in 2 cm (¾ in) pieces
1 small cauliflower, cut into 2 cm (¾ in) pieces
½ tsp ground turmeric
⅓ tsp chili powder
1 tsp ground cumin
2 tomatoes, chopped
1 tsp salt
¼ tsp sugar
200 g (7 oz) peas
½ tsp Garam Masala see page 113

1 Heat the oil in a large saucepan over medium high heat. Add the onions and fry for 3–4 minutes until light brown.

2 Add the potatoes and cauliflower and stir. Add the spices, tomatoes, salt and sugar. Stirfry for 2–3 minutes.

3 Add the peas, cover and lower heat to medium low and cook for about 20 minutes until the potatoes and cauliflower are tender. Stir the vegetables a few times to stop them sticking. Sprinkle with Garam Masala before serving.

Carrots with Yogurt

Serves 4–6
450 g (1 lb) carrots, sliced
1 tsp sugar
½ tsp ground cumin
1 small onion, finely chopped
juice ½ lemon
150 ml (5 fl oz) yogurt
salt and freshly ground black pepper

1   Cook the carrots with the sugar in boiling water just until they are al dente. Drain them and add the cumin and onion. Stir.
2   Mix the lemon juice into the yogurt, season to taste and spoon it over the carrots.
3   Serve immediately or leave it to cool and serve as a salad or an accompaniment to curry.

Grated Carrot and Cabbage

Serves 4
2 tbsp oil
1 tsp mustard seeds
1 head collard greens, finely shredded
450 g (1 lb) carrots, grated
a little honey
salt and freshly ground black pepper

1   Heat oil in a heavy-based saucepan with a lid. When it is hot, add the mustard seeds.
2   As soon as the mustard seeds begin to pop, add the shredded vegetables, drizzle over the honey and stir well. Turn down the heat, put on the lid and cook for 3 minutes or until just tender. Season and serve.

Green Beans with Baby Corn

Serves 4–6
225 g (8 oz) green beans, washed
    and trimmed
225 g (8 oz) baby corn
3–4 tbsp oil
1½ tsp salt
1 tsp sugar
2 tbsp/30 ml (1 fl oz) water

1   Depending on the size of the baby corn, leave them whole if small, or cut them into two or three diamond-shaped pieces if larger.
2   Heat a wok or large frying pan over high heat until very hot, add the oil and swirl it so that the cooking surface is well greased. When the oil starts to smoke, add the beans and baby corn and stirfry for about 1 minute.
3   Add the salt and sugar and continue stirring for another minute or so. Add the water if the vegetables dry out before they are cooked.
4   Serve as soon as all the liquid has evaporated. If you prefer your vegetables slightly underdone, serve when there is just a little liquid left in the wok.

Stirfried Asparagus

Serves 4

450 g (1 lb) asparagus
2 tbsp oil
1 tsp salt
1 tsp sugar

1 Wash the asparagus well in cold water and discard the tough ends of the stalks.
2 Heat the oil in a very hot wok or frying pan, swirling it to grease the pan well. Add the asparagus when the oil starts smoking. Stirfry until each piece is coated with oil.
3 Add salt and sugar and continue stirring for 1–1½ minutes only. No extra liquid should be added as it would spoil the color and texture.
4 This dish can be served either hot or cold.

Hot and Sour Cabbage

Serves 6
700 g (1½ lb) white cabbage
5 small dried red chilies
2 tbsp soy sauce
1½ tbsp vinegar
1½ tbsp sugar
1½ tsp salt
3 tbsp sunflower oil
10 Sichuan peppercorns
1 tsp sesame oil

1 Choose a round, pale green cabbage with a firm heart—never use loose-leafed cabbage. Wash in cold water and cut the leaves into small pieces the size of a matchbox.
2 Cut the chilies into small pieces. Mix the soy sauce, vinegar, sugar and salt to make the sauce.
3 Heat the sunflower oil in a preheated wok until it starts to smoke. Add the peppercorns and the red chilies and a few seconds, later the cabbage. Stir for about 1½ minutes until it starts to go limp.
4 Pour in the prepared sauce and continue stirring for a short while to allow the sauce to blend in. Add the sesame seed oil just before serving. This dish is delicious both hot and cold.

Stirfried Green and Red Peppers

Serves 4
1 large or 2 small green peppers, cored and seeded
1 large or 2 small red peppers, cored and seeded
3 tbsp oil
1 tsp salt
1 tsp sugar

1 Cut the peppers into small diamond-shaped pieces; if you use one or two orange peppers, the dish will be even more colorful.
2 Heat the oil in a hot wok or large frying pan until it smokes. Spread the oil with a spatula so that the cooking surface is well greased. Add the peppers and stirfry until each piece is coated with oil. Add salt and sugar.
3 Continue stirring for about 1 minute and serve if you like your vegetables crunchy and crisp. If not, you can cook them for another minute or so until the skin of the peppers becomes slightly wrinkled. Add a little water if necessary during the last stage of cooking.

Chestnuts and Vegetables

Serves 6–8

450 g (1 lb) chestnuts
4 tbsp olive oil
2 fat cloves garlic, chopped
175 g (6 oz) mushrooms, sliced
350 g (12 oz) Brussels sprouts
350 g (12 oz) red cabbage
salt and freshly ground black pepper
small glass red wine

1 Preheat the oven to 200°C/400°F/Gas Mark 6. Make a nick in the top of the chestnuts with a sharp knife and boil them for 10 minutes. Plunge them in cold water and peel.
2 Heat the olive oil in a flameproof casserole dish and fry the garlic. Add the mushrooms, sprouts and red cabbage and season. Cook, stirring occasionally, for about 5 minutes until coated with oil and beginning to soften.
3 Stir in the chestnuts and red wine. Cover and bake in the oven for 40 minutes. Serve with baked potatoes or a Purée of Root Vegetables (see page 104).

Savory Vegetable Julienne

Serves 4

1 tbsp sunflower oil
1 green chili, seeded and finely chopped
1 clove garlic, crushed
½ head fennel, cut into thin strips
1 leek, cut into thin strips
1 green pepper, cut into thin strips
¼ small red cabbage, shredded
1 tbsp lemon juice
salt and freshly ground black pepper

1 Heat the sunflower oil in a large saucepan and add the chili and garlic. Cook for 1–2 minutes, then add the fennel, leek, pepper and cabbage.
2 Stir-fry for 3–4 minutes. Add the lemon juice and season to taste.

Roasted Cauliflower

Serves 4

4 medium tomatoes
1 large onion
3 cloves garlic
1 cm (½ in) fresh ginger
2 tbsp ghee (see page 113)
¾ tsp ground turmeric
½ tsp chili powder
½ tsp garam masala (see page 113)
175 g (6 oz) peas
½ tsp salt
1 medium-sized cauliflower, blanched

1 Blend the tomatoes, onion, garlic and ginger until you have a paste.
2 Heat the ghee in a frying pan over medium heat and add the paste, turmeric, chili and garam masala and stirfry until the ghee and spices separate, about 5–6 minutes.
3 Add the peas and salt and cook for 5 minutes, stirring constantly. Remove from the heat.
4 Place the cauliflower in a large ovenproof dish and pour the spices over it. Place in a preheated oven at 190°C/375°F/Gas Mark 5 for 30–35 minutes. Serve on a flat plate with the peas and spices poured over.

Green Beans in Garlic Sauce

Serves 4

400 g (14 oz) stringless green beans
1 large or 2 small cloves of garlic
3 tbsp oil
1 tsp salt
1 tsp sugar
1 tbsp light soy sauce

1 Trim the beans. Leave them whole if they are young and tender; otherwise, cut them in half. Crush and finely chop the garlic.

2 Blanch the beans in a saucepan of lightly salted boiling water, drain and plunge in cold water to stop the cooking and to preserve the beans' bright green color. Drain.

3 Heat the oil in a hot wok or frying pan. When it starts to smoke, add the crushed garlic to flavor the oil. Before the color of the garlic turns dark brown, add the beans and stirfry for about 1 minute. Add the salt, sugar and soy sauce and continue stirring for another minute at most. Serve hot or cold.

Purée of Root Vegetables

Serves 4
175 g (6 oz) carrots
175 g (6 oz) rutabaga
1 turnip
1 parsnip
salt and freshly ground black pepper
butter

1 Trim and peel the vegetables and simmer in salted water until tender.
2 Drain and mash into a fluffy purée with butter. Season with salt and plenty of black pepper. Serve with a dish that has a crunchy texture, such as Chestnuts and Vegetables (see page 102) or Nut Loaf (see page 74).

Corn Croquettes

Serves 4
3 tbsp butter
3 tbsp flour
300 ml (10 fl oz) milk
salt and freshly ground
    black pepper
1–2 tbsp finely
    chopped parsley
400 g (14 oz) corn,
    cooked
2 egg yolks

Coating
2 eggs, beaten
seasoned flour
fine stale breadcrumbs
oil for frying

1 To make the sauce, cut the butter into small pieces and melt in a heavy-bottomed saucepan. Stir in the flour and cook for a few minutes until the mixture is a pale gold.
2 Remove from the heat and pour in the milk. Stir well, return to the heat and stir until the sauce has thickened. Season with salt and plenty of pepper.
3 Stir the parsley, corn and egg yolks into the mixture. Chill.
4 The mixture should have a heavy dropping consistency. Form it into croquettes. Dip each in the beaten egg, then roll in the flour and breadcrumbs.
5 Fry the croquettes in oil until crisp.

Cheese and Potato Croquettes

Serves 6–8
900 g (2 lb) potatoes
2 egg yolks
4 tbsp butter
salt and freshly ground black pepper
pinch nutmeg
dash sherry
100 g (4 oz) grated Parmesan cheese
pinch mustard powder
2 tbsp chopped parsley
seasoned flour
egg wash (egg beaten with a little milk)
breadcrumbs

1 Wash and peel the potatoes, and cut to an even size. Cook in salted water until soft, then drain.
2 Put a lid on the saucepan of the potatoes and place over low heat to dry out, stirring occasionally to prevent burning.
3 Place the potatoes in a food processor with the egg yolks, butter and seasoning.
4 Mix in the nutmeg, sherry, Parmesan cheese, mustard and parsley. The potatoes should be like a very firm mash. Overmixing will make them gluey, in which case some flour will have to be worked in by hand.
5 Check that the mixture is seasoned well and mold into cylinder shapes (13 x 5 cm/5 x 2 in).
6 Roll in seasoned flour; dip in eggwash and coat with breadcrumbs.
7 Deep fry in hot fat, 185°C/365°F. When golden, drain well and serve.

Fennel Mornay

Serves 4
3 bulbs fennel
bay leaf

Sauce
2 tbsp butter
25 g (1 oz) plain unbleached flour
300 ml (10 fl oz) milk
150 ml (5 fl oz) half and half
100 g (4 oz) Cheddar cheese, grated
25–50 g (1–2 oz) breadcrumbs
salt and freshly ground black pepper

1 Trim the fennel and simmer in salted water with a bay leaf for about 30 minutes until tender.
2 Meanwhile, make the sauce. Melt the butter in a saucepan and stir in the flour. Cook, stirring, for a couple of minutes and then gradually stir in the milk. Add the cream and most of the cheese and cook gently until the cheese has melted. Season well and keep warm.
3 Drain the fennel and cut each bulb in half. Lay the halves in a flameproof dish and pour the sauce over them. Sprinkle with the remaining cheese and the breadcrumbs. Broil to brown and melt the cheese.

Cook's Tip
For a tangier sauce, add a little powdered English mustard to taste.

Patatas Bravas

Serves 2–3

1 onion, chopped
2 tbsp olive oil
1 bay leaf
2 red chilies
2 tsp finely chopped garlic
1 tbsp tomato purée
½–1 tbsp sugar
1 tbsp soy sauce
400 g (1 lb) can plum tomatoes, chopped
1 glass white wine
salt and freshly ground black pepper
3 medium potatoes
melted butter

1 Sweat the onion in the oil with the bay leaf.
2 When soft, add the chilies, garlic, tomato purée, sugar and soy sauce. Sweat for a further 5 minutes on low heat.
3 Add the chopped tomatoes and white wine. Stir and bring to a boil. Simmer for 10 minutes. Taste and season. (This sauce should be slightly sweet; the flavor of the tomatoes should not dominate it).
4 Cut the potatoes like small roast potatoes. Grease a baking tray. Season the potatoes well and brush with melted butter.
5 Roast in a hot oven, 230°C/450°F/Gas Mark 8, until golden. Serve with the tomato sauce for dipping.

Russian Potatoes

Serves 6–8

900 g (2 lb) potatoes
salt and freshly ground black pepper
4 tbsp butter
1 large onion, sliced
100 g (4 oz) mushrooms, sliced
200 ml (7 fl oz) sour cream
3 tbsp chopped chives

1 Scrub the potatoes and cook in salted water until barely tender. Drain, peel and slice.

2 Heat some of the butter in a flameproof casserole and fry the onion until translucent. Add the mushrooms and cook gently until the juices run. Add the rest of the butter as necessary and stir in the potatoes. Let them gently brown on one side, season, turn over and add the sour cream.

3 When most of the sour cream has been absorbed, sprinkle over the chopped chives and a little more pepper and serve.

Split Peas with Vegetables

Serves 4–6

200 g (7 oz) split peas, washed
750 ml (1½ pt) water
2 tbsp ghee (see page 113)
½ tsp whole cumin seeds
2 bay leaves
2–3 green chilies, cut lengthways
275 g (10 oz) diced potatoes, cut into
   2.5 cm (1 in) pieces
75 g (3 oz) peas
350 g (12 oz) cauliflower, cut into large florets
½ tsp ground turmeric
1 tsp salt

1 In a large saucepan, bring the split peas and water to a boil. Cover and simmer for 30 minutes. Remove from heat.

2 Heat the ghee in a large saucepan over medium high heat. Add the cumin seeds, bay leaves and green chilies and let them sizzle for a few seconds.

3 Add the potatoes, peas and cauliflower and fry for 1–2 minutes.

4 Add the boiled split peas with the water, turmeric and salt. Mix thoroughly, lower the heat and cook until the vegetables are tender. (If it gets too thick add a little more water).

Black-eyed Peas with Onions

Serves 4–6

200 g (7 oz) black-eyed peas, washed
1.1 litre (2½ pt) water
2 tbsp oil
1 large onion, finely chopped
2 cloves garlic, crushed
5mm (¼ in) fresh ginger, grated
1–2 green chilies, finely chopped
½ tsp salt
1 tsp corn syrup

1 Soak the black-eyed peas in the water overnight.
2 Boil the black-eyed peas in the water and then cover and simmer for 1 hour until tender. Drain.
3 Heat the oil in a large saucepan and fry the onion, garlic, ginger and chili until the onions are soft. Add the black-eyed peas, salt and corn syrup and cook until all the moisture is absorbed, about 15 minutes. Serve with Baktora Yogurt Bread (page 144).

Egg-fried Rice

Serves 6–8

3 eggs
2 scallions, finely chopped
1 tsp salt
4 tbsp oil
100 g (4 oz) peas
600 g (20 oz) cooked rice
1 tbsp light soy sauce (optional)

1 Lightly beat the eggs with about half of the scallions and a pinch of salt.
2 Heat about half of the oil in a hot wok or frying pan, pour in the beaten eggs and lightly scramble until set. Remove.
3 Heat the remaining oil and when hot, add the remaining scallions followed by the peas and stir-fry for about 30 seconds. Add the cooked rice and stir to separate each grain. Add the salt and soy sauce together with the eggs and stir to break the eggs into small pieces. Serve as soon as everything is well blended.

Perfect Boiled Rice

Serves 4

275 g (10 oz) long-grain rice
600 ml (1 pt) water

1 Wash and rinse the rice in cold water until clean.
2 Bring the water to a boil in a saucepan over high heat. Add the washed rice and bring back to the boil. Stir the rice with a spoon to prevent it sticking to the bottom of the saucepan and then cover the saucepan tightly with a lid and reduce the heat to very low. Cook gently for 15–20 minutes.

Cook's Tip
It is best not to serve the rice immediately. Fluff it up with a fork or spoon and leave it under cover in the saucepan for 10 minutes or so before serving.

Chow Mein–Fried Noodles

Serves 4

25 g (1 oz) dried tofu sticks
25 g (1 oz) dried tiger lily buds
50 g (2 oz) bamboo shoots
100 g (4 oz) spinach, or any other greens
1 green pepper
225 g (8 oz) dried egg noodles
3–4 tbsp oil
2 scallions, thinly shredded
2 tbsp light soy sauce
1 tsp salt
2 tsp sesame oil

1 Soak the dried vegetables overnight in cold water or in hot water for at least an hour. When soft, thinly shred both the tofu skins and tiger lily buds.

2 Shred the bamboo shoots and greens into thin strips. Cook the noodles in a saucepan of boiling water according to the instructions on the packet. Depending on the thickness of the noodles, this should take 5 minutes or so. Freshly made noodles will take only about half that time.

3 Heat about half of the oil in a hot wok or frying pan. While waiting for it to smoke, drain the noodles in a sift. Add them with about half of the scallions and the soy sauce to the wok and stirfry. Do not overcook, or the noodles will become soggy. Remove and place them on a serving dish.

4 Add the rest of the oil to the wok. When hot, add the other scallions and stir a few times. Then add all the vegetables and continue stirring. After 30 seconds or so, add the salt and the remaining soy sauce, and a little water if necessary. As soon as the gravy starts to boil, add the sesame oil and blend everything well. Place the mixture on top of the fried noodles as a dressing.

Vegetarian Special Fried Rice

Serves 4

4–6 dried Chinese mushrooms
1 green pepper, cored and seeded
1 red pepper, cored and seeded
100 g (4 oz) bamboo shoots
2 eggs
2 scallions, finely chopped
2 tsp salt
4–5 tbsp oil
900 g (30 oz) cooked rice
1 tbsp light soy sauce (optional)

1 Soak the dried mushrooms in warm water for 25–30 minutes, then squeeze dry and discard the hard stalks. Cut the mushrooms into small cubes.
2 Cut the green and red peppers and the bamboo shoots into small cubes.
3 Lightly beat the eggs with about half of the scallions and a pinch of the salt.
4 Heat about 2 tbsp of oil in a hot wok, add the beaten eggs and scramble until set. Remove.
5 Heat the remaining oil. When hot, add the rest of the scallions followed by all the vegetables and stirfry until each piece is covered with oil. Add the cooked rice and salt and stir to separate each grain of rice. Finally add the soy sauce (optional), blend everything together and serve.

Fried Rice

Serves 4

3 tbsp ghee (see page 113)
2 bay leaves
5 cm (2 in) cinnamon stick
4 green cardamom pods
3 large onions, finely sliced
3 green chilies, cut lengthways
350 g (12 oz) basmati rice, cooked and cooled
1 tsp salt
½ tsp sugar
2 tbsp raisins (optional)

1 Heat the ghee in a large frying pan over medium high heat. Add the bay leaves and spices; let them sizzle a little.
2 Add the onions and chilies and fry until the onions are golden brown. Add the rice, salt, sugar and raisins and continue frying until the rice is thoroughly heated through.

Pilaf Rice with Coconut

Serves 4–6

325 g (12 oz) basmati rice, rinsed and drained

2 tbsp dried coconut

2–3 green chilies

1 tsp salt

½ tsp sugar

2 tbsp raisins

1 tbsp pistachio nuts, skinned and cut into
thin strips

5 cm (2 in) cinnamon stick

4 green cardamom pods

3 tbsp Ghee (see page 113)

600 ml (1 pt) milk

275 ml (10 fl oz) water

1   Mix the rice with all the dry ingredients.
2   Heat the ghee in a large saucepan over medium heat. Add the rice mixture and sauté for 5 minutes, stirring constantly.
3   Add the milk and water, increase the heat to high and bring to a boil. Stir.
4   Lower heat to very low, cover and cook for about 20 minutes until all the liquid has evaporated. Fluff the pilaf with a fork and serve hot.

SAUCES AND DRESSINGS

Sauces and dressings are invaluable to the vegetarian cook, since they can turn a plainly prepared vegetable or salad into something altogether more interesting. They can save time—and vitamins—allowing the vegetables to be lightly cooked or served raw, and then dressed.

Ghee (Clarified Butter)

Makes about 450 ml (¾ pt)
450 g (1 lb) unsalted butter

1 Heat the butter in a saucepan over low heat. Let it simmer for 15–20 minutes until all the white residue turns golden and settles at the bottom.
2 Remove from the heat, strain and cool. Pour into an airtight bottle and store in a cool place.

Garam Masala

Makes about 4 tbsp
3 tbsp cardamom seeds
7.5 cm (3 in) cinnamon stick
½ tbsp cumin seeds
½ tsp black peppercorns
½ tsp cloves
¼ nutmeg

1 Finely grind all the spices together. Store in a spice bottle until required. (The ingredients may be added in different proportions to suit individual tastes).

Tahini Dip

Makes 400 ml (14 fl oz)
250 ml (8 fl oz) tahini
4 tbsp water
4 tbsp lemon juice
3 cloves garlic, crushed
pinch salt

1 Put the tahini in a small bowl and stir in the water and lemon juice. Add in the crushed garlic and salt.

Yogurt

Makes about 1.1 litre (2 pt)
1.1 l (2½ pt) milk
2 tbsp plain live yogurt at room temperature

1 Scald the milk. Heat it until it is ready to boil. Just before the boiling point, remove the saucepan from the heat and leave to cool until lukewarm. Test by dripping a little milk on your wrist. It should feel warm, not hot.
2 Put the yogurt in the chosen container and stir in a little milk until smooth. Now stir in the remaining milk.
3 Cover and place container in the incubator. Be careful not to disturb the yogurt for about 4 hours. When the consistency is right, chill in the fridge to set before using.

Cook's Tip
Yogurt can be made in any sterile container with a tightly fitting lid inside any sort of incubator, such as an oven with the pilot light on or a Styrofoam box, but as the secret of successful yogurt making is a constant lukewarm temperature, it is best to use a special yogurt maker. Don't put incubating yogurt near a heat source regulated by a thermostat that switches on and off. Use 2 tbsp of the homemade yogurt to start the next batch. The cost of making yogurt at home is minimal and the method is easy.

Mayonnaise

Makes 400 ml (14 fl oz)

2 egg yolks
½ tsp salt
1 tsp Dijon mustard
300 ml (½ pt) olive oil
2 tsp cider vinegar

1   All the ingredients must be at room temperature. Put the egg yolks in a bowl with the salt and mustard and whisk together, or use a food processor.

2   Beating constantly and evenly, add the olive oil at a very slow trickle. A bottle with a nick cut in the cork can be used to ensure that only a very little oil dribbles out at a time. The aim is to break up the oil into very small globules so that it can be absorbed by the egg yolks. When all the oil has been added you should have a thick glossy emulsion that will cling to the whisk.

3   Gradually beat in the cider vinegar. For a thinner mayonnaise, beat in 1 tbsp hot water.

Mayonnaise Maltaise

Makes 400 ml (14 fl oz)
400 ml (14 fl oz) mayonnaise (see above)
grated rind and juice of 2 oranges

1 Combine the ingredients and serve with cooked vegetables such as asparagus and artichokes, or use as a salad dressing.

Green Mayonnaise

Makes 350 ml (12 fl oz)
3 tbsp chopped fresh spinach
3 tbsp chopped watercress
3 tbsp chopped scallion
3 tbsp chopped parsley
250 ml (8 fl oz) Mayonnaise (see opposite page)
½ tsp grated nutmeg
salt

1 Put the spinach, watercress, scallion and parsley in a small saucepan. Add water to cover them.
2 Quickly bring to a boil. Remove the saucepan from the heat. Let stand for 1 minute.
3 Drain the greens well. Rub them through a sift or purée them in a blender. Drain off excess liquid.
4 Put the mayonnaise in a blender or medium-sized bowl. Add the purée, nutmeg and salt to taste. Blend until evenly mixed.

Yogurt Mayonnaise

Makes 250 ml (8 fl oz)
120 ml (4 fl oz) plain yogurt
1 tbsp honey
1 tsp fresh lemon juice
4½ tbsp Mayonnaise (see opposite page)
¼ tsp salt
1 tsp poppy seeds

1 Combine the yogurt, honey and lemon juice in a bowl. Stir with a wooden spoon until well blended.
2 Add the mayonnaise, salt and poppy seeds. Stir until thoroughly mixed. Chill for 1 hour and serve.

Béchamel Sauce

Makes about 900 ml (1½ pt)
600 ml (1 pt) milk
1 small onion, peeled
1 small carrot, peeled and sliced
1 bay leaf
6 slightly crushed peppercorns
1 blade mace
1 stalk parsley
3 tbsp butter
6 tbsp flour
salt and freshly ground white pepper

1 Pour milk into a saucepan. Add the onion, cut into quarters, with 2 slices of carrot, the bay leaf, peppercorns, mace and parsley stalk.
2 Cover and warm on low heat without boiling for about 10 minutes. Remove from the heat and allow to infuse for a further 10 minutes, covered.
3 Make a roux (a blend of butter and flour) by melting the butter in a saucepan. Do not allow the butter to brown. Add the flour and stir well over a medium heat.
4 Gradually add the strained milk and stir briskly or whisk until a smooth creamy sauce is made; then season to taste.

Hot Tomato Sauce

Makes about 400 ml (14 fl oz)
1 tbsp oil
1 onion, finely chopped
2–3 cloves garlic, finely chopped
400 g (15 oz) can tomatoes, mashed, with juice
2 tbsp tomato paste
1 tsp ground cumin
1 tsp ground cilantro
½ tsp chili powder
salt

1 Heat the oil in a saucepan, add onion and garlic and stirfry until soft.
2 Add remaining ingredients, simmer until thickened and check seasoning. Serve with Vegetable Couscous (page 84).

Marinara Sauce

Makes about 1.1 l (1¾ pt)
4 tbsp olive oil
2 cloves garlic, crushed
1½ kg (3 lb) ripe beef tomatoes, peeled
    and roughly chopped
salt and freshly ground black pepper
6 basil leaves

1 Heat the oil in a saucepan, add the garlic and stir-fry for 1 minute. Add the tomatoes and seasoning and let simmer for 6 minutes.
2 Chop the basil leaves and add to the tomatoes, then stir the sauce for one more minute. Serve on freshly cooked pasta. This sauce is a simple accompaniment to pasta, which is very good to eat and easy to prepare. The secret is that the tomatoes should be simply heated through, not cooked to a pulp.

Cucumber Dill Sauce

Makes about 600 ml (l pt)
1 medium cucumber, peeled
2 tbsp butter
150 ml (¼ pt) vegetable stock
150 ml (¼ pt) dry white wine
2 tbsp fresh dill, chopped or 1 tbsp dried dill
4 tsp cornstarch
2 tbsp water
120 ml (4 fl oz) sour cream or yogurt
salt and pepper

1 Coarsely grate the cucumber and put it into a saucepan. Add the butter and cook on a gentle heat just to soften the cucumber. Add the stock, wine and dill and simmer for 5 minutes. Mix the cornstarch with the water. Add it to the saucepan, cook gently until the sauce begins to thicken, stirring constantly. Add the sour cream or yogurt and warm it through. Season to taste.
2 Serve hot or cold, with poached eggs, boiled potatoes, rice or pasta.

Creamy Mustard Vinaigrette

Makes about 150 ml (¼ pt)

3 tbsp olive oil

2 tbsp whipping cream

2 tbsp red wine vinegar

1 tbsp Dijon-style mustard

½ tsp dried thyme

1½ tsp soy sauce

salt and freshly ground black pepper

1 Put the olive oil, cream, vinegar and mustard in a bowl. Stir with a fork or whisk until the mixture is somewhat foamy. Stir in the thyme, soy sauce, salt and pepper.

Light Vinaigrette

Makes 250 ml (8 fl oz)

2 tbsp wine vinegar

1 tbsp lemon juice

1 tsp mustard

salt and freshly ground black pepper

175 g (6 fl oz) extra-virgin olive oil

1 Put the vinegar, lemon juice, mustard, salt and pepper in a jar with a tightly fitting lid.

2 Cover the jar tightly and shake until the salt dissolves. Add the olive oil to the jar and shake until well mixed.

Rich Vinaigrette

Makes about 400 ml (14 fl oz)

1 egg

120 ml (4 fl oz) oil

2 tbsp lemon juice

1 clove garlic, crushed

fresh herbs

salt and freshly ground black pepper

250 ml (8 fl oz) yogurt

1 Blend together the egg, oil, lemon juice, garlic, herbs, salt and pepper. Slowly add the yogurt, with the blender running. Refrigerate until needed—the vinaigrette should thicken as it stands.

Cook's Tip

This makes a delicious salad dressing but if you want to make it thicker, for piping, you can add some gelatin and let it set. Try adding chives, fennel, parsley, tarragon or any other fresh herb you have to hand—or a mixture.

Blue Cheese Dressing

Makes about 400 ml (14 fl oz)
250 ml (8 fl oz) yogurt
50 g (2 oz) blue cheese
3 tbsp olive oil
salt and freshly ground black pepper

1 Place the yogurt in a bowl and add the blue cheese.
2 Stir in the olive oil and season with salt and pepper.

Tomato Dressing

Makes 175 ml (6 fl oz)
4 tbsp tomato paste
3 tbsp olive oil
4 tbsp lemon juice
2 cloves garlic, crushed
1 small onion, finely chopped
1 tbsp honey
pinch salt

1 Add to a bowl the olive oil, tomato paste, garlic and onion. Stir in the lemon juice and honey.
2 Season with salt.

Sour Cream Dressing

Makes about 150 ml (¼ pt)
150 ml (5 fl oz) sour cream
1 clove garlic, crushed
3 scallions, finely chopped
chopped dill
juice of 1 lemon
salt and freshly ground black pepper

1 Mix everything together well. Refrigerate until needed.
2 Serve as a salad dressing.

Basil Dressing

Makes 250 ml (8 fl oz)
250 ml (8 fl oz) yogurt
10 basil leaves, finely chopped
1 large clove garlic, crushed
salt and freshly ground black pepper

1 Blend everything together well. Serve over green or mixed salad or tomato and onion salad.

Cook's Tip
This also makes a good sauce for pasta, in which case double the quantity.

Herb Dressing

Makes 350 ml (12 fl oz)
75 g (3 oz) cream cheese
250 ml (8 fl oz) yogurt or buttermilk
salt and freshly ground black pepper
finely chopped fresh herbs

1 Blend everything together well. Refrigerate until needed.
2 Serve as a salad dressing.

Lemon Dressing

Makes 175 ml (6 fl oz)
1 tsp water
large pinch salt
large pinch grated lemon zest
2 tsp dried mint
4 tbsp fresh lemon juice
120 ml (4 fl oz) extra-virgin olive oil
large pinch ground black pepper

1 Put the water, salt and lemon zest in a jar with a tightly fitting lid. Let stand for 2 minutes.
2 Add the mint and lemon juice. Cover the jar tightly and shake.
3 Add the olive oil and black pepper. Cover the jar tightly, shake again and serve.

Thousand Island Dressing

Makes 325 ml (11 fl oz)
250 ml (8 fl oz) Mayonnaise (see page 114)
4 tbsp Tabasco or chili sauce
2 tbsp finely chopped pimento-stuffed
   green olives
1 hard-boiled egg, finely chopped
1 tbsp whipping cream
½ tsp fresh lemon juice
1½ tsp finely chopped scallion
2 tbsp finely chopped green pepper
2 tbsp finely chopped fresh parsley
¼ tsp paprika
large pinch freshly ground black pepper

1 Put the Mayonnaise and chili sauce in a medium-sized bowl. Stir with a wooden spoon until well blended.
2 Add the olives, egg, cream and lemon juice. Continue stirring.
3 Add the remaining ingredients. Stir until well blended. Refrigerate for at least 1 hour before serving. This dressing well on tossed green salad.

Chutney Dressing

Makes about 350 ml (12 fl oz)
120 ml (4 fl oz) sour cream
120 ml (4 fl oz) buttermilk
2 tbsp mango chutney
1 tbsp lemon juice
2 tsp extra-virgin olive oil
2 tsp Dijon-style mustard
salt and freshly ground black pepper

1 Blend everything together well. Refrigerate until needed.
2 Serve on salad or cold vegetables.

Fruit Salad Syrup Dressing

Makes 300 ml (½ pt)
1 tbsp flour
150 ml (5 fl oz) water
½ tsp pure vanilla extract
1 egg
5 tbsp sugar
2 tsp butter
large pinch ground nutmeg
3 tbsp whipping cream

1 Put the flour and 2 tbsp water into a saucepan. Stir to form a thin paste. Add the vanilla and egg. Beat well until smooth.
2 Put the sugar, remaining water and butter in another saucepan. Bring to a boil over low heat.
3 Add the boiling syrup to the vanilla and egg mixture. Stir well. Cook over low heat, stirring constantly, until thick and smooth.
4 Remove the saucepan from the heat. Allow the dressing to cool.
5 Stir in the nutmeg and cream. Beat until well blended and pour over the fruit salad.

DRINKS, PICKLES AND CHUTNEYS

The emphasis on healthy eating—and less alcohol consumption—has bought the attractions of fresh fruit drinks to a wider public, while pickles and chutneys are a much-treasured legacy from earlier days. The following recipes are the stock of an international pantry.

Mint and Chili Cucumber

Makes 325 ml (11 fl oz)

1 cucumber, grated, sprinkled with salt and
    placed in a sift to remove excess moisture
1 beef (large) tomato, peeled
½ tsp garlic, chopped
bunch mint, chopped
150 ml (5 fl oz) plain yogurt
150 ml (5 fl oz) sour cream
1 tsp cumin
2 red chilies, seeded and chopped
salt and freshly ground black pepper

1 Wash the excess moisture off the cucumber and
   drain well, squeezing any moisture out. Chop the
   tomato into little squares; discard the seeds.
2 Mix all the ingredients together in a bowl, season
   well and chill.

Mint Chutney

Makes 250 ml (8 fl oz)

50 ml (2 fl oz) tamarind juice
50 g (2 oz) mint leaves, washed
2 tbsp onions, chopped
2 cloves garlic
2 cm (¾ in) root ginger
2–3 green chilies
½ tsp salt
½ tsp sugar

1 Make the tamarind juice by soaking 1 dried
   tamarind in boiling water for 10 minutes.
2 Blend all the ingredients together until you have a
   smooth paste. Serve with any fried foods (Can be
   stored in an airtight jar in the fridge for one week).

Cilantro Chutney

Makes 300 ml (½ pt)

75 g (3 oz) cilantro leaves
4 cloves garlic
3 tbsp dried coconut
2 green chilies
2–3 tbsp lemon juice
½ tsp salt
¼ tsp sugar

1 Chop the sprigs of cilantro and throw away the
   roots and lower stalk.
2 Blend the cilantro with all the other ingredients
   until you have a smooth paste. Serve with any fried
   foods. (Can be stored in an airtight jar in the fridge
   for one week).

Fresh Tomato, Cucumber and Onion Sambal

Makes about 750 ml (1½ pt)

225 g (8 oz) tomatoes, chopped into 5 mm
 (¼ in) pieces
225 g (8 oz) cucumber, cut into 5 mm
 (¼ in) pieces
100 g (4 oz) onions, chopped
2–3 green chilies
½ tsp salt
¼ tsp sugar
3 tbsp lemon juice
2 tbsp cilantro leaves, chopped

1 Mix all the ingredients together in a small bowl. Cover and set aside to chill. Serve with any Indian meal.

Cucumber Raita

Makes about 600 ml (1 pt)

½ cucumber, peeled and chopped
1 small onion, chopped
500 ml (17 fl oz) yogurt
squeeze lemon juice
salt and freshly ground black pepper
cilantro leaves

1 Mix all the ingredients together, seasoning to taste, and garnish with the cilantro leaves. Use parsley if cilantro is not available.
2 Chill well before serving.

Pineapple Chutney

Makes about 250 ml (8 fl oz)

½ tbsp sunflower oil
½ tsp whole mustard seeds
235 g (8 oz) canned pineapple, crushed
 and drained
big pinch salt
1 tsp cornstarch mixed with a little milk

1 Heat the oil in a small saucepan over medium heat. Add the mustard seeds and let them sizzle for a few seconds.
2 Add the drained pineapple and salt and, stirring occasionally, cook for about 10 minutes.
3 Thicken with the cornstarch mixture and remove from the heat. Chill.

Pickled Radishes

Serves 4–6
24 radishes
2 tsp sugar
1 tsp salt

1 Choose fairly large radishes that are roughly equal in size, if possible, and cut off and discard the stalks and tails. Wash the radishes in cold water and dry them thoroughly. Using a sharp knife, make several cuts from the top about two-thirds of the way down the sides of each radish.
2 Put the radishes in a large jar. Add the sugar and salt. Cover the jar and shake well so that each radish is coated with the sugar and salt mixture. Leave to marinate for several hours or overnight.
3 Just before serving, pour off the liquid and spread out each radish like a fan. Serve them on a plate on their own or as a garnish with other cold dishes.

Chinese Pickled Vegetables

Use four to six of the following vegetables, or more:

cucumber	garlic
carrot	4.5 l (9½ pt) cold
radish or turnip	boiled water
cauliflower	175 g (6 oz) salt
broccoli	50 g (2 oz) chilies
green cabbage	3 tsp Sichuan
white cabbage	peppercorns
celery	60 ml (2 fl oz) Chinese
onion	distilled spirit (or
fresh ginger	white rum, gin
leek	or vodka)
scallion	100 g (4 oz) root ginger
red pepper	100 g (4 oz)
green pepper	brown sugar
green beans	

1 Put the cold boiled water into a large, clean earthenware or glass jar. Add the salt, chilies, peppercorns, spirit, ginger and sugar.
2 Wash and trim the vegetables, peel if necessary, and drain well. Put them into the jar and seal it, making sure it is airtight. Place the jar in a cool place and leave the vegetables to pickle for at least five days before serving.
3 Use a pair of clean chopsticks or tongs to pick the vegetables out of the jar. Do not allow any grease to enter the jar. You can replenish the vegetables, adding a little salt each time. If any white impurities appears on the surface of the brine, add a little sugar and spirit. The longer the pickling lasts, the better.

Caution
It is very improtant to be aware of hygiene when pickling any food product. Seek further advice from experts.

Sloe Gin

Makes 1 bottle
ripe sloes, washed
the best Dutch gin

1 Half fill a bottle with sloes and fill it to the top with gin. Seal the bottle and store in a dark place.
2 The gin will take on a beautiful pink color and a tangy fruity flavor within about two weeks. You can leave it longer if you want a stronger, fruitier taste, or you can decant the gin and top up the bottle with fresh gin a second time. Sloe gin makes an ideal Christmas drink.

Tomato Cocktail

Serves 4
3–4 medium/450 g (1 lb) ripe tomatoes, skinned
300 ml (10 fl oz) yogurt
fresh basil
salt and freshly ground black pepper
pinch sugar
2 ice cubes

1   Squeeze out the seeds of the tomatoes (reserve them for use in a soup) and place the flesh in a blender, together with the remaining ingredients. Blend everything together well. Serve immediately in tall glasses. Garnish with additional basil leaves.

Green Beech Liqueur

Makes 1 bottle
tender young beech leaves
vodka
fruit sugar
brandy

1   Pick young beech leaves in late spring or early summer. Make sure they are tender. (What you don't use in this recipe you can eat in a salad).
2   Pack the leaves into a jar and press them down. Fill the jar with vodka. Seal and leave for two weeks in a dark place.
3   Strain off the vodka, which will now be bright green color.
4   To make the liqueur, prepare a syrup of 225 g (8 oz) fruit sugar and 300 ml (10 fl oz) boiling water to every 500ml (1pt) of vodka. Stir the sugar into the water until dissolved. When cool, add 1 tbsp brandy for each 300 ml (10 fl oz) of water and sugar and combine with the vodka. Bottle and seal.

Orange Yogurt Drink

Serves 2
175 ml (6 fl oz) yogurt
120 ml (4 fl oz) milk
grated rind and juice of 1 orange
grated lemon peel
1 tsp honey
1½ tbsp ground hazelnuts (optional)

1   Blend all the ingredients together well.
2   Serve immediately or refrigerate until needed.

BREADS AND PASTRIES

Bread comes in many colors and textures, as do sweet and savory biscuits, rolls and muffins, yeast pastries, tarts and cakes. The plethora of ingredients available today allows the home baker to create an exceptional range of breads and pastries.

Whole Wheat Bread

Makes 1 loaf

450 g (1 lb) whole wheat flour

2 tbsp seeds (sesame, caraway or poppy)

1½ heaped tsp salt

300 ml (½ pt) warm water

15 g (½ oz) fresh yeast or 7 g (⅓ oz) dried yeast

1 tbsp oil

1 tbsp malt extract

½ tsp corn syrup

beaten egg to glaze

1 tsp seeds (sesame, caraway or poppy) to top the loaf

1 Mix the flour, seeds and salt together in a warm bowl. Pour a little of the water into a small bowl and add the yeast. Put in a warm place for 10 minutes. If using dried yeast, make according to the manufacturer's instructions.

2 Add the oil, malt extract and corn syrup to the rest of the water in a jug.

3 Pour the yeast mixture into the flour and stir. Add enough of the other liquid to make a soft dough, but don't let it get too sticky. As different brands of flour absorb different amounts, it may not be necessary to add all this liquid, so don't add it all at once. Gather it with your hands into a ball.

4 Knead the dough for 20 minutes, then place in a greased plastic bag to rise. Put it in a warm place, such as a sunny window sill. Leave it there for an hour.

5 Preheat the oven to 200°C/400°F/Gas Mark 6. Punch down the dough with the heel of your hand to redistribute the rising agent and knead it for a minute. Put it in an oiled loaf pan 22 x 12 cm (8½ x 4½ in). Brush the top with beaten egg and sprinkle over the remaining seeds. Cover the loaf with a clean damp dish towel and leave it to rise on top of the stove.

6 Bake for 35 minutes. Take out of the pan and flick the bottom of the loaf with your fingernail. It should sound hollow. The sides of the loaf should spring back when pressed. Let it cool on a wire rack.

Walnut bread

Add 50 g (2 oz) roughly chopped walnuts to the flour and use walnut oil instead of olive oil. Omit the corn syrup. This loaf will fill the kitchen with its delicious nutty aroma and taste marvellous with jam for breakfast. Or try Cheddar and watercress sandwiches in walnut bread with tomato soup for supper.

Marmite bread

Omit the corn syrup and replace the malt extract with Marmite. Add 1–2 tbsp caraway seeds to the flour and sprinkle the top of the loaf with the seeds. This bread is good with strong Cheddar or simply with butter as an accompaniment to a lunchtime bowl of soup.

Quick White Bread

Makes 2 large or 4 small loaves

2 tbsp/50 g (2 oz) fresh yeast or 4 tbsp/dried
    yeast and ½ tsp sugar
750 ml (1½ pt) warm water
2 x 25 mg tablets vitamin C
1.5 kg (3 lb) white flour
2 tsp salt
2 tbsp sugar
50 g (2 oz) butter or margarine

1   Preheat the oven to 230°C/450°F/Gas Mark 8.
2   Grease two large (or four small) bread pans. Mix the yeast with a few tbsp water, adding 1 tsp sugar if dried yeast is used. Set the dried yeast liquid aside for 10 minutes until frothy. Crush the vitamin C tablets in a little water; add to the yeast liquid.
3   Mix the flour and salt together in a large warm bowl. Add the sugar and rub in the fat. Stir in the yeast liquid and the rest of the warm water and mix into a soft dough. Turn onto a lightly floured board and knead the dough until it is smooth, elastic and non-sticky. Divide the dough in half, shape into 2 or 4 loaves and put them into the bread pans. Cover the pans with plastic wrap and let rise until doubled in size, about 1 hour.
4   Remove the plastic wrap and bake the loaves for about 45 minutes (30–35 minutes for small loaves). Cool the bread on a wire rack.

White Bread

Makes 3 large loaves

1 tbsp fresh yeast or 2 tbsp dried yeast and
    1 tsp sugar
900 ml (2 pt) warm water
1.5 kg (3 lb) white flour
2–3 tsp salt
1 tbsp sugar
50 g (2 oz) butter or margarine

1   Preheat the oven to 230°C/450°F/Gas Mark 8.
2   Grease three large bread pans. Stir the yeast with a few tbsp water, adding 1 tsp sugar if dried yeast is used. Put the bowl of dried yeast liquid aside for 10 minutes until frothy.
3   Mix the flour and salt together. Add the sugar, rub in the fat, stir in the yeast liquid and the rest of the warm water to make a soft dough. Turn the dough onto a lightly floured board and knead until it becomes smooth, elastic and non-sticky.
4   Return the dough to the bowl, cover it with plastic wrap and let it rise until doubled in size, about 1½ hours.
5   Knock back the dough and divide it into 3 portions. Knead and shape into loaves to fit into the three bread pans. Cover the bread pans with plastic wrap. Let it rise until doubled in size, about 45 minutes.
6   Remove the film and bake the loaves for 45–50 minutes. Cool on a wire rack.

White and Brown Rolls

Cob loaf

Shape the dough into a large ball. Flatten it slightly and place on a greased baking sheet. Slash the top of the dough with a sharp knife to make a cross. Cover and let rise for about 45 minutes in a warm place. Bake for 30–40 minutes.

Rolls (makes 12)

Baking time for rolls is 10–15 minutes after shaping, proving and glazing.

Clover leaf rolls

Divide each 50 g (2 oz) piece of dough into 3 equal parts. Shape into 3 balls. Place on the baking sheet in the shape of a clover leaf and press lightly together.

Two-strand braided rolls

Divide the 50 g (2 oz) dough pieces in half. Roll each piece into a strand 20 cm (8 in) long. Place the strands in the form of a cross on the work surface. Take the two ends of the lower strand and cross them over the middle of the upper strand so that they lie side by side. Repeat this with the remaining strand and repeat alternately until all the dough has been used. Pinch the ends firmly together. Place on the baking sheet, glaze and decorate, cover, let rise and bake.

Three-strand braided rolls

Cut off 50 g (2 oz) pieces of risen dough. Divide and roll each piece into three 10 cm (4 in) strands and braid.

Knot rolls

Roll 50 g (2 oz) pieces of dough into a thick 15 cm (6 in) strand. Tie into a simple knot.

Braid

Divide the dough into three equal pieces. Roll each piece into a strand 30–35 cm (12–14 in) long. Pinch together one end of the three strands and then braid them. Pinch the remaining ends together and lift the braid onto a greased baking sheet. Cover, let rise and glaze. Decorate with poppy seeds, if desired. Bake for 25–30 minutes.

Milk Bread

Makes 2 loaves

15 g (½ oz) fresh yeast or 1 package dried yeast and ½ tsp sugar
450 ml (15 fl oz) warm skim milk or whole milk and water, mixed
675 g (1½ lb) white flour
1½ tsp salt
1½ tsp sugar
6 tbsp butter or margarine
beaten egg or milk for glazing

1 Preheat the oven to 200°C/400°F/Gas Mark 6.
2 Grease 1 large and 1 small bread pan. Stir the yeast into the liquid, adding sugar if dried yeast is used. Allow 15 minutes in a warm place for dried yeast to become frothy.
3 Mix the flour, salt and sugar and rub in the butter or margarine. Stir in the yeast liquid and mix into a soft dough. Turn the dough onto a lightly floured board and knead until it becomes smooth and loses its stickiness. Return the dough onto the warm mixing bowl and cover it with oiled plastic wrap. Leave to rise until doubled in size, about 1½ hours.
4 Knock back the dough, divide it into 1 large and 1 small piece and shape to fit the bread pans. Brush the loaves with beaten egg or milk. Cover the pans with oiled plastic wrap and allow to rise until doubled in size, about 1 hour. Bake for about 50 minutes and cool on a wire rack.

Olive bread

Omit the 1½ tsp sugar and stir in 5–6 tbsp olive oil instead of rubbing in the butter or margarine. Add 225 g (½ lb) stoned, sliced black olives to the dough with the dough liquid. The olive loaves can be shaped into two or three rounds and baked on greased baking trays instead of being baked in bread pans.

Bagels

Makes 18

25 g (1 oz) fresh yeast or 15 g dried yeast and
  ½ tsp brown sugar
450 ml (15 fl oz) warm milk
1 tsp brown sugar
50 ml (2 fl oz) vegetable oil
2 tsp salt
550 g (1¼ lb) whole wheat flour (a little extra
  may be needed)
2 l (4 pt) water
2 tbsp brown sugar
eggwash for glazing [1 egg yolk plus 1 tbsp water]
toasted sesame seeds, poppy seeds, or
  sautéed chopped onions for decoration

1 Preheat the oven to 190°C/375°F/Gas Mark 5.
2 Grease two baking sheets. Dissolve the yeast in
  the warm milk, adding the sugar if dried yeast is
  used. Allow about 10 minutes for dried yeast to
  rehydrate and the liquid to become frothy.
3 Add the brown sugar, oil and salt to the yeast
  liquid and work in the flour slowly, beating at first
  and then kneading the stiffer dough. When all the
  flour has been incorporated, knead the dough on
  a floured board for 10 minutes. Return the dough
  to the warm bowl, cover with oiled plastic wrap
  and let rise for about 1 hour until doubled in size.
  Knock back the dough, cover and let rise until
  doubled in size once again.
4 Knock back the dough and divide it into 18 equal
  pieces. Roll each piece into a strand 15 cm (6 in)
  long, 2.5 cm (1 in) thick, tapering at each end.
  Shape into rings, pinching the ends firmly together.
  Cover the shaped bagels and let rise for 10–15
  minutes. Bring the water to a boil and add the
  2 tbsp brown sugar.
5 Put two or three bagels at a time into the boiling
  water and cook until they rise to the surface (takes
  1 or 2 minutes). Lift out the bagels with a perforated
  spoon. Place them on the greased baking sheets.
  Glaze the bagels with egg wash and sprinkle with
  seeds or onions.
6 Bake until browned, about 20 minutes.

Onion Bread

Makes 1 round loaf

one-quarter of the Quick White Bread
  dough (page 130)
225 g (8 oz) onions, sliced
50 g (2 oz) butter or margarine
2 tbsp/15 g (½ oz) white flour
150 ml (5 fl oz) milk
¼ tsp salt or garlic salt
pinch freshly ground black pepper
1 tsp poppy or sesame seeds

1 Preheat the oven to 190°C/375°F/Gas Mark 5.
2 Grease and flour a round cake pan 20 cm (8 in) in
  diameter. Roll out the dough to fit the pan. Put the
  dough into the pan, cover with plastic wrap and let
  rise until doubled in size, about 30 minutes.
3 Cook the onions in the fat in a heavy-based
  saucepan until transparent and softened. Stir in
  the flour and cook for a couple of minutes. Add the
  milk, stirring constantly. Bring to a boil and simmer
  for another minute. Add the salt and pepper.
4 Spread the onion mixture over the dough and
  sprinkle with the seeds. Bake for 30 minutes. Serve
  hot or cold with soup or salad.

Potato Bread

Makes 3 loaves

1 large raw potato
450 ml (¾ pt) milk
30 g (1 oz) fresh yeast or 1 package dried yeast
    and 1 tsp sugar
900 g (2 lb) flour
2 tsp salt
1 egg
3 tbsp sour cream

1 Preheat the oven to 180°C/350°F/Gas Mark 4.
2 Grease 3 16 x 9 x 7.5 cm (6½ x 3½ x 3 in) bread
   pans. Grate the peeled potato finely. Bring the milk
   to a boil and pour it over the potato in a bowl. Cool
   until lukewarm and add the fresh yeast. If dried
   yeast is used stir it, with the sugar, into 3 tbsp
   warm milk or water and leave for 8–10 minutes
   until frothy.
3 Add the dried yeast mixture to the potato–milk
   mix. Beat in half the flour until well mixed. Add the
   salt, egg, sour cream and the rest of the flour. Beat
   the mixture thoroughly.
4 Cover the bowl with plastic wrap and set aside in
   a warm place for 2–2½ hours. Knead thoroughly
   and divide between the three bread tins.
5 Let rise once again, covered, for about 40 minutes.
   Bake for 45 minutes until cooked.

Oatmeal Bread

Makes 2 small loaves

25 g (1 oz) fresh yeast or 1 package dried yeast
   and 1 tsp brown sugar

550 ml (18 fl oz) warm water

25 g (1 oz) strong plain bread flour

2 tbsp brown sugar

500 g/1 lb/2 oz/ mixed flour (½ whole wheat,
   ½ white flour)

175 g (6 oz) oats (fine oatmeal)

4 tbsp wheatgerm

4 tbsp soya flour

2 tbsp/30 ml (1 fl oz) vegetable oil

1½ tsp salt

1 Preheat the oven to 180°C/350°F/Gas Mark 4.
Grease two small bread tins. Put the yeast into
a bowl (with the sugar, if dried yeast is used)
and stir in 120 ml (4 fl oz) of the warm water.
Set aside for up to 10 minutes until foamy. Add
the strong plain bread flour, sugar and half the
mixed flours to the rest of the water and beat
well for 5 minutes. Add the yeast liquid and beat
thoroughly. Stir in the oatmeal and set the mixture
aside in a warm place for about 30 minutes to
make a sponge batter.

2 Add the wheatgerm, soya flour, oil, salt and the
rest of the mixed flours to the sponge batter. Turn
out onto a floured board and knead well until
smooth. Return the dough to the bowl and cover
with oiled plastic wrap. Set aside in a warm place
until doubled in size, about 30 minutes.

3 Knock back the dough on a floured board and
divide into two pieces. Shape into loaves and
place them in the bread tins. Cover with oiled
plastic wrap and allow to rise until double in
size once again. Bake for about 1 hour. Cool
on a wire rack.

Iced Buns

Makes 8 rolls
15 g (½ oz) fresh yeast or 10 g (⅓ oz) dried yeast
   and 1 tsp sugar
150 ml (5 fl oz) warm milk
225 g (8 oz) white flour
2 tsp sugar
½ tsp salt
2 tbsp/25 g (1 oz) butter or margarine

Glacé icing
175 g (6 oz) powdered sugar
3 tbsp/45 ml (1½ fl oz) water
coloring (optional)

1 Preheat the oven to 220°C/425°F/Gas Mark 7.
2 Grease one or two baking sheets (depending on size). Stir the yeast with the milk, adding 1 tsp of sugar if using dried yeast. If the latter, allow the yeast liquid to stand for 10 minutes or so until frothy.
3 Mix the flour with the sugar and salt and rub in the fat. Stir in the yeast liquid and mix into a soft dough. Turn onto a lightly floured board and knead thoroughly until the dough loses its stickiness and becomes smooth. Return the dough to the warm bowl, cover with oiled plastic wrap and let rise until doubled in size, about 1 hour.
4 Knock back the dough, divide it into 8 pieces and shape each piece into an oblong 12 cm (5 in) long.
5 Place the rolls on the greased baking sheet(s). Cover with oiled plastic wrap and let rise prove in a warm place for about 20 minutes. Uncover the rolls and bake for about 15 minutes until browned. Lift onto a wire rack to cool. Combine the icing ingredients and ice the rolls with it.

Cornbread

Makes 16 squares
100 g (4 oz) whole wheat flour
100 g (4 oz) corn meal
½ tsp salt
1 tsp baking soda
¾ tsp cream of tartar
350 ml (12 fl oz) buttermilk or half yogurt,
   half skim milk
3 tbsp sunflower oil
2 eggs, beaten
1 tbsp brown sugar or honey

1 Preheat the oven to 220°C/425°F/Gas Mark 7.
2 Grease a 20 cm (8 in) square baking pan. Mix together the flour, corn meal, salt, baking soda, and cream of tartar. Stir the buttermilk with the oil, eggs and sugar or honey. Pour the liquid ingredients into the dry mixture and stir together.
3 Pour the batter into the pan and bake for about 35 minutes. Cut into 5 cm (2 in) squares and serve warm.

Cheese Bread

Makes 1 large loaf
15 g (½ oz) fresh yeast or 10 g (⅓ oz) dried yeast
   and ½ tsp sugar
300 ml (10 fl oz) warm water
450 g (1 lb) white flour
1 tsp salt
¼ tsp cayenne pepper
½ tsp mustard powder or 2 tsp
   creamed horseradish
2 tbsp chives
1 tbsp butter or margarine
100 g (4 oz) finely grated Cheddar cheese
beaten egg or milk for glazing
1–2 tbsp grated cheese for decorating (optional)

1   Preheat the oven to 200°C/400°F/Gas Mark 6.
2   Grease one large or two small bread pans. Stir the
    yeast into the warm water, adding sugar if dried
    yeast is used.
3   Stand the dried yeast liquid for 10 minutes to
    become frothy.
4   Put the flour, salt, cayenne pepper, mustard and
    chives into a bowl and rub in the fat. Stir in the
    cheese and then the yeast liquid (and horseradish,
    if used). Work together to make a dough. Turn
    the dough onto a floured board and knead until
    smooth and non-sticky.
5   Return to the bowl, cover with plastic wrap and
    leave to rise for 1 hour until doubled in size. Knock
    back the dough and shape into 1 large or 2 small
    loaves. Place the shaped dough in the pan. Brush
    the dough with beaten egg or milk. Cover the pan
    with plastic wrap and let rise in a warm place for
    about 45 minutes.
6   Sprinkle the dough with grated cheese, if desired.
7   Bake for about 40 minutes until brown. Turn out
    and cool the bread on a wire rack.
8   This bread makes delicious toast and may be
    used as a quick pizza base.

Irish Soda Bread

Makes 1 loaf
450 g (1 lb) all-purpose flour
1 tsp salt
2 tsp baking soda
1½ tsp cream of tartar
2 tbsp lard
300 ml (½ pt) buttermilk

1   Preheat the oven to 220°C/425°F/Gas Mark 7.
2   Sift the flour, salt, baking soda and cream of tartar
    into a bowl. Rub in the lard and add enough
    buttermilk to make a soft dough. Turn the mixture
    onto a lightly floured board and knead for a
    minute. Shape into a round and place on the
    baking sheet. Mark with a cross, cutting deep into
    the dough.
3   Bake for 40–50 minutes, until lightly browned and
    firm when tapped on the base. Cool the bread on
    a wire rack.

Variations
You can use plain milk instead of buttermilk, but if
you do, double the quantity of cream of tartar. You can
also use a mixture of white and whole wheat flours.

Italian Panettone

Makes 1 loaf

25 g (1 oz) fresh yeast or 15 g (½ oz) dried yeast
   and 1 tsp sugar
175 ml (6 fl oz) warm milk
450 g (1 lb) strong plain bread flour
1 tsp salt
5 tbsp sugar
5 tbsp butter
2 eggs plus 2 egg yolks, beaten
2 tsp ground cardamom
zest of 2 small lemons, finely grated
75 g (2½ oz) mixed dried citrus peel, chopped
100 g (4 oz) raisins, chopped and soaked in
   2 tbsp rum
beaten egg for glazing

1 Grease a deep, round cake pan, 20 cm (8 in) in diameter. Stir the yeast into the milk, adding 1 tsp of sugar if dried yeast is used. Set the dried yeast liquid aside for about 10 minutes until frothy. Add a quarter of the flour to the yeast liquid and set aside in a warm place for ½ hour. Add to the yeast batter the rest of the flour, the melted butter, the beaten eggs and egg yolks, cardamom, lemon zest, mixed peel and the raisins in rum. Mix thoroughly to form a heavy dough. Knead well, cover with oiled plastic wrap and leave to rise for 1½–2 hours.

2 Knock back the dough and knead well. Put the dough into the greased cake pan. Brush the top of the loaf with eggwash. Cover with oiled plastic wrap and let rise for about 40 minutes

3 Preheat the oven to 200°C/425°F/Gas Mark 7 and bake for 20 minutes, then reduce the temperature290°C/375°F/Gas mark 5 for 30 minutes.

4 Turn out of the pan after 10 minutes and cool on a wire rack.

Walnut, Apricot and Orange Bread

Makes 1 large or 2 small loaves

15 g (½ oz) fresh yeast or 10 g (⅓ oz) dried
    yeast and 1 tsp honey
300 ml (½ pt) warm water
450 g (1 lb) whole wheat flour
50 g (2 oz) sugar
1 tsp salt
50 g (2 oz) butter or margarine
50 g (2 oz) chopped walnuts
175 g (6 oz) dried apricots, soaked and chopped
2 tbsp grated orange rind

1 Preheat the oven to 220°C/425°F/Gas Mark 7.
2 Grease one large or two small bread pans.
   Dissolve the yeast (and sugar) in the warm water
   leaving the dried yeast to become frothy (10 to 15
   minutes). Mix the flour with the sugar and salt and
   rub in the fat. Stir in the yeast liquid and mix into
   a dough. Turn onto a floured board and knead
   until smooth. Return the dough to the bowl, cover
   it with oiled plastic wrap and let it rise for about
   1 hour until doubled in size. Knead again, working
   in the nuts, apricots and orange rind. Shape into
   a loaf (or 2 loaves) and place them in the prepared
   pan(s). Cover the dough and let rise once more for
   40–50 minutes.
3 Bake for about 45–50 minutes, depending on the
   size of the loaf (loaves).
4 Leave to cool on a wire rack.

Swiss Pear Bread

Makes 1 large loaf or 2 small loaves

1 kg (2 lb) dried pears
225 g (8 oz) golden raisins
100 g (4 oz) hazelnuts, chopped
6 tbsp thick candied lemon peel, finely diced
225 g (8 oz) sugar
7 tsp/110 ml (4½ fl oz) rosewater
½ glass Kirsch
1 tbsp powdered cinnamon
900 g (2 lb) Quick White Bread dough (see page
    130)

1 Preheat the oven to 220°C/425°F/Gas Mark 7.
2 Grease two baking sheets.
3 Soak the pears overnight in water to cover, then
   stew them in the water in which they were soaked.
4 Drain and mash the pears, removing any stems
   or cores. Mix the mashed pears with the golden
   raisins, nuts, lemon peel, sugar, rosewater, Kirsch
   and cinnamon. Knead half the bread dough
   with the pear mixture and shape into two oblong
   loaves.
5 Roll out the other half of the dough on a floured
   board. Divide it in half and wrap each pear loaf
   inside a sheet of plain dough. Brush the edges
   of the dough with milk and seal them. Prick the
   loaves with a fork. Bake for 50–60 minutes.

Almond Bread

Makes about 4–5 slices
350 g (12 oz) white flour
2 tsp baking powder
¼ tsp salt
2 large eggs
120 ml (4 fl oz) sunflower oil
5–6 tbsp honey or brown sugar
2 tsp grated orange or tangerine rind
2 tsp almond extract
100 g (4 oz) chopped almonds

1   Preheat the oven to 180°C/350°F/Gas Mark 4.
2   Sift the flour, baking powder and salt together. Beat together in an electric blender or a bowl the eggs, oil, honey, citrus rind and almond extract. Transfer the mixture into a large bowl and beat in the flour mixture a little at a time.
3   Stir the almonds into the stiff dough, then divide it into six oblong rolls about 5 cm (2 in) wide. Space the rolls apart on a foil-covered baking sheet and bake for 20 minutes.
4   Lift out the baking sheet and cut each roll into seven or eight slices 1 cm (½ in) thick. Return the slices to the oven and bake for 15–20 more minutes until brown. Cool on a wire rack.

English Muffins

Makes 12
15 g (½ oz) fresh yeast or 10 g (⅓ oz) dried yeast and 1 tsp honey
250 ml (8 fl oz) warm milk
450 g (1 lb) white flour
1 tsp salt
2 tbsp butter, melted
2 small eggs, beaten

1   Preheat the oven to 230°C/450°F/Gas Mark 8. Grease two baking sheets and dust them well with oats, wheat germ, corn meal or semolina. Or heat a greased and floured griddle (or heavy frying pan) if the muffins are to be cooked on top of the stove.
2   Stir the yeast into the warm milk, adding the honey if dried yeast is used. Set the dried yeast liquid aside for 10 minutes until foamy.
3   Mix the flour and salt and add the yeast liquid, melted butter and the eggs. Mix into a soft dough in the bowl then turn it out onto a floured board. Knead the dough until it becomes smooth, non-sticky and elastic. Return the dough to the warm bowl. Cover with oiled plastic wrap and let rise for about 1¼ hours, until doubled in size. Turn the dough onto a lightly floured surface, knead and then roll the dough to 1 cm (½ in) thickness. Cover with oiled plastic wrap and rest for 5 minutes. Cut into 7.5 cm (3 in) rounds with a plain cutter.
4   Put the muffins on the baking sheets and dust the tops with semolina. Cover with oiled plastic wrap and leave to rise for about 40 minutes. Cook the muffins by baking them in the oven for about 10 minutes, turning them over with a palette knife after 5 minutes. Or cook the muffins for 5 minutes on each side on the heated griddle. Stack the muffins on a wire rack.
5   To serve the muffins, pull them open all around the edges. Leave the halves joined in the center. Toast them slowly on both sides. Pull the muffins fully apart and place a slice of chilled butter inside. Put the halves together again and serve them hot.

Oatcakes

Makes about 22

100 g (4 oz) soft brown sugar
50 g (2 oz) unbleached flour
100 g (4 oz) whole wheat flour
100 g (4 oz) oatmeal
pinch baking soda
pinch salt
8 tbsp butter
1 egg yolk

1 Preheat the oven to 180°C/350°F/Gas Mark 4. Mix the dry ingredients together in a bowl. Cut the butter into small pieces in the bowl and rub in with your fingertips.

2 Mix in the egg yolk and form into a dough. Knead for a few minutes and then roll out thinly on a lightly floured surface and cut into rounds with a pastry cutter.

3 Leaving plenty of space between each one, arrange the rounds on a greased baking sheet and bake for 10–15 minutes until crisp and golden. Leave to cool slightly before transferring to a wire rack. When cool, store in an airtight tin. Serve with cheese.

Crumpets

15 g (½ oz) fresh yeast or 1 pack of dried yeast and ½ tsp sugar
300 ml (½ pt) warm water
350 g (12 oz) white flour
1 tsp salt
½ tsp baking soda
200 ml (7 fl oz) warm milk (more, if required, to make a pouring batter)

1 Heat a greased griddle or heavy frying pan. When ready to cook the batter, grease crumpet rings, egg-poaching rings or plain pastry cutters 75 mm (3 in) in diameter. Stir the yeast into the water, adding the sugar if dried yeast is used.

2 Let the dried yeast liquid stand for 5–10 minutes until frothy. Mix in half of the flour and beat well. Set the batter aside in a warm place for about 30 minutes until foamy.

3 Add the rest of the ingredients to the batter, stirring in thoroughly. Beat well, adjusting the milk quantity if necessary.

4 Place the crumpet rings on the heated griddle and pour 2 tbsp batter into each ring. Cook until set underneath and holes appear on the upper surface. Take away the rings and turn the crumpets with a spatula. Lightly cook the second side. Cool the crumpets stacked on a wire rack. Serve freshly made with butter, or toast them on both sides, later serving them hot with butter.

Pita Bread

Makes 8

Use the same ingredients and follow the recipe for Whole Wheat Bread, up to and including step 4 (page 129).

1 Preheat the oven to 230°C/450°F/Gas Mark 8. Punch down the dough with the heel of your hand and knead for a minute. Divide the dough into eight and roll out into thin ovals. Place on baking sheets and cover with clean damp cloths. Leave on top of the stove for 20 minutes.
2 Bake for 5–7 minutes. Leave to cool. These pita breads freeze well.

Bran and Sultana Muffins

Makes 12
2 tbsp/30 ml (1 fl oz) oil
2 tbsp/30 ml (1 fl oz) honey
1 egg
150 ml (5 fl oz) milk
125 g (5 oz) whole wheat flour
75 g (3 oz) bran
2 tsp baking powder
pinch salt
50 g (2 oz) golden raisins

1 Pre-heat the oven to 190°C/375°F/Gas Mark 5. Beat the oil and honey together. Beat in the egg. Gradually beat in the milk until smooth.
2 Combine the dry ingredients and stir these into the liquid mixture. When the bran has soaked up the liquid, you should have a soft dough.
3 Spoon into an oiled muffin pan and bake for about 20 minutes.

Spiced Buttermilk Scones

Makes 8
225 g (8 oz) unbleached flour
225 g (8 oz) whole wheat flour
2 tsp baking soda
2 tsp cream of tartar
1 tsp fruit sugar
1 tsp mixed spice
3 tsp baking powder
8 tbsp/100 g (4 oz) butter
300 ml (10 fl oz) buttermilk

1 Preheat the oven to 220°C/425°F/Gas Mark 7. Sift the flours together and mix thoroughly with the other dry ingredients. Cut the butter into the flour mix and rub in well.
2 Stir in the buttermilk and mix to form a soft dough. Knead the dough lightly on a floured board. Divide in half, form each half into a round and cut each round into four wedges. Place the wedges on a greased baking sheet, dust with flour and bake for about 12 minutes.
3 Cool on a wire rack. While still warm, slice in half and fill with butter and jam.

Sesame Snaps

Makes about 20
100 g (4 oz) whole wheat flour
50 g (2 oz) sesame seeds
1 tsp baking powder
1–2 tsp salt
2 tsp tahini paste
1 tbsp olive oil
3–5 tbsp lukewarm water

1 Preheat the oven to 220°C/425°F/Gas Mark 7. Combine the dry ingredients in a bowl. Add the tahini and olive oil and mix with your fingertips until crumbly. Gradually add enough water to form a soft dough.
2 Knead gently on a floured board and then roll out thinly. Press out rounds with a pastry cutter and arrange on a greased baking sheet. Bake in the oven for 15 minutes until crisp and golden.
3 Cool on a wire rack, store in a tin and serve with cheese.

Rye Savory Biscuits

Makes about 20
2 tbsp butter
100 g (4 oz) rye flour
pinch salt
a little milk, heated

1 Preheat the oven to 180°C/350°F/Gas Mark 4. Rub the butter into the flour with a pinch of salt, and bind with a little milk to form a dough. Knead for about 7 minutes.
2 Form the dough into about 20 small balls and roll flat on a floured surface.
3 Bake on a baking sheet for about 10 minutes, until the edges are just beginning to brown. Cool on a wire rack. Store in a tin and serve with butter and cheese.

Indian Lucchi Bread

Makes about 40
350 g (12 oz) all-purpose flour
½ tsp salt
2 tbsp oil
175 ml (6 fl oz) hot water
oil for deep frying

1 Sift the flour and salt together. Rub in the oil. Slowly add enough water to form a stiff dough. Knead for about 10 minutes until you have a soft, pliable dough.
2 Divide the dough into about 40 small balls and flatten each ball.
3 Roll out a few balls on a slightly oily surface into rounds of 10 cm (4 in) across (do not roll out all the balls at the same time as they tend to stick).
4 Heat oil in a large saucepan or cast-iron frying pan over high heat. Put in a lucchi and press the middle with a slotted spoon so it will puff up. Turn and cook the other side for a few seconds. Drain and serve hot.

Stuffed Potato Paratha

Makes about 20
450 g (1 lb) potatoes, boiled and mashed
1 small onion, finely chopped
1–2 green chillies, finely chopped
1 tbsp cilantro leaves, chopped
¾ tsp salt
¾ tsp ground roasted cumin

Dough
325 g (12 oz) all-purpose flour
½ tsp salt
4 tbsp oil
175 ml (6 fl oz) hot water
ghee (see page 113) for frying

1 Mix all the ingredients for the filling together and set aside.
2 To make the dough, sift the flour and salt together. Rub in the oil. Add enough water to form a stiff dough. Knead for about 10 minutes until you have a soft, smooth dough. Divide into 20 balls.
3 Roll out two balls into 10 cm (4 in) rounds each. Place about 1½–2 tbsp of the filling on one of the rounds and spread it evenly. Place the other round over the filling, sealing the edges with a little water.
4 Roll out gently into 18 mm (1 in) rounds, and be careful that no filling comes out. Roll out all the parathas in a similar manner.
5 Heat a frying pan over medium heat. Place a paratha in the frying pan and cook for about 1 minute until brown spots appear. Turn and cook the other side.
6 Add 2 tsp ghee and cook for 2–3 minutes until golden brown. Turn and cook the other side, adding more ghee if required. Make all the parathas in the same way. Serve warm.

Naan Bread

Makes 12

1 tsp dried yeast
1 tsp sugar
75 ml (2½ fl oz) lukewarm water
275 g (10 oz) all-purpose flour
½ tsp salt
¾ tsp baking powder
1 tbsp oil
about 3 tbsp plain yogurt

1   Stir the yeast and sugar into the water and set aside for 15–20 minutes until frothy.
2   Sift together the flour, salt and baking powder. Make a well in the middle, add the yeast liquid, oil and yogurt and knead for about 10 minutes until soft and not sticky.
3   Place the dough in a plastic bag and leave in a warm place for 2-3 hours, until doubled in size.
4   Knead again for 1–2 minutes and divide into 12 balls. Roll into 18 cm (7 in) rounds.
5   Place as many as possible on a baking sheet and put in a preheated oven at 200°C/400°F/Gas Mark 6 for 4–5 minutes each side until brown spots appear. Broil them for a few seconds until slightly browned. Keep warm to serve (see below).

Baktora Yogurt Bread

Makes 12–14

225 g (8 oz) all-purpose flour
1½ tsp baking powder
½ tsp salt
1 tsp sugar
1 egg, beaten
about 3 tbsp yogurt
oil for deep frying

1   Sift the flour, baking powder and salt together. Mix in the sugar.
2   Add the beaten egg and enough yogurt to form a stiff dough. Knead for 10–15 minutes until you have a soft, smooth dough. Cover with a cloth and let it rest for 3–4 hours.
3   Knead again on a floured surface for 5 minutes. Divide into 12–14 balls.
4   Roll out on a floured surface into 12.5 cm (5 in) rounds.
5   Heat the oil in a large saucepan over high heat. Fry each baktora, pressing in the middle with a slotted spoon so that it puffs up. Turn and cook the other side for a few seconds until lightly browned.

Zucchini and Cream Cheese Loaf

Makes 1 loaf
4 baby zucchini
1 egg, beaten
4 tbsp oil
2 tbsp honey
2 tbsp corn syrup
2 tbsp cream cheese
175 g (6 oz) whole wheat flour
50 g (2 oz) soya flour
pinch salt
2 tsp baking powder
1 tsp baking soda

1 Preheat the oven to 170°C/325°F/Gas Mark 3. Cut the zucchini into thin strips, leaving on the skin, then cut into 1 cm (½ in) pieces.
2 Put the egg in a bowl and beat in the oil, honey and corn syrup. Beat in the cream cheese until smooth.
3 In another bowl, combine the dry ingredients, stirring well. Mix in the zucchini. Gradually stir the dry ingredients into the cream cheese mixture.
4 Transfer batter to a greased and floured loaf pan and bake for 50–60 minutes.

Amaretti Cookies

Makes about 20
2 egg whites
100 g (4 oz) fruit sugar
100 g (4 oz) ground almonds
1 tsp Kirsch (optional)
few drops vanilla extract
rice paper sheets

1 Preheat the oven to 180°C/350°F/Gas Mark 4. Whisk the egg whites until they form soft peaks. Gradually add the sugar, whisking continuously until the mixture is thick and lustrous. Stir in the ground almonds, Kirsch and vanilla.
2 Line baking trays with sheets of rice paper. Take a spoonful of mixture about the size of a plum and roll it into a ball in the palms of your hands. With a sticky mixture, you will find it easier if your hands are wet. Flatten the balls and arrange them on the baking trays with plenty of space for them to expand during cooking.
3 Bake for 20–30 minutes. Leave to cool slightly, then carefully remove biscuits with their rice paper bases (which are edible) and cool them completely on a wire rack. Store in an airtight tin. (see below).

Hazelnut and Apricot Crunch

Makes about 16
8 tbsp butter
50 g (2 oz) soft brown sugar
2 tbsp maple syrup
100 g (4 oz) oats
50 g (2 oz) chopped hazelnuts
50 g (2 oz) dried apricots, chopped

1 Preheat the oven to 180°C/350°F/Gas Mark 4. Put the butter, sugar and syrup in a heavy-based saucepan and stir over low heat until combined.
2 Stir in the remaining ingredients. Press into a jelly roll pan lined with parchment paper. Bake for about 45 minutes, until golden. Cut into bars in the pan using an oiled knife. Cool in the pan.

Muesli Cookies

Makes 15–20
175 g (6 oz) golden raisins
50 g (2 oz) dried apricots, chopped
1 egg, beaten
2 tbsp butter, melted
2 tbsp hot water
175 g (6 oz) muesli
1 heaped tbsp chopped nuts

1 Preheat the oven to 180°C/350°F/Gas Mark 4. Pick over dried fruit and wash in boiling water. Drain. In a bowl, beat the fruit with egg and butter. Stir in muesli and nuts.
2 Line a biscuit tray with parchment paper and spread the mixture thinly over it. Mark into fingers and bake for 45 minutes.
3 Cut fingers through and leave to cool for 10 minutes before removing from the tray. Finish cooling on a wire rack.

Shortcrust Pastry

100 g (4 oz) flour
pinch salt
4 tbsp butter or a mixture of butter and
    margarine
2 tbsp cold water

1   Sift the flour and salt into a bowl. Cut up the butter
    and crumble it into the flour. Mix in just enough
    water with a knife to make a firm dough and
    gather it into a ball. On a floured surface, knead
    the dough gently until smooth. Wrap it in plastic
    wrap and refrigerate for a short while to firm.

2   To line a pie plate, roll out the pastry on a floured
    surface to a thickness of 2.5–5 mm (1/8 – 1/4 in)
    and about 5 cm (2 in) bigger than the pie plate.
    Grease the pie plate and lay the pastry gently in it,
    pressing it down to fit the bottom and sides. Prick
    the bottom lightly and leave to rest in a cool place
    for 30 minutes.

Whole wheat Pastry

75 g (2½ oz) whole wheat flour
75 g (2½ oz) whole wheat self-rising flour
pinch salt
6 tbsp polyunsaturated margarine
water

1   Mix the flours and salt together in a bowl. Cut the
    fat into small pieces in the flour and rub in with
    your fingertips until the mixture is fine and crumbly.
    Add enough water to bind together and roll into
    a smooth ball. Chill in the fridge for 20 minutes.

2   To use, roll the pastry out on a floured surface.

Sour cream Pastry

275 g (10 oz) flour
scant 200 g (7 oz) butter or margarine
1 egg
1 tbsp rum (optional)
2 tbsp sour cream
75 g (3 oz) superfine sugar

1   Rub the flour and butter together. Mix in the remaining ingredients to make a firm dough. Knead well and let it rest for half an hour before using.
2   This is excellent for any pie or tart that requires a sweet pastry. You can make delicious cookies from any trimmings when using the pastry (or make some especially for cookies).

Cheese Pastry

225 g (8 oz) cottage cheese
100 g (4 oz) butter
100 g (4 oz) margarine
225 g (8 oz) flour
1 tsp baking powder

1   Mix the cheese and fats together and rub them into the flour and baking powder.
2   Refrigerate for at least 3 hours.

Yogurt Pastry

100 g (4 oz) butter or margarine, cut into
   small pieces
175 g (6 oz) flour
1 tsp baking powder
75 ml (3 oz) yogurt

1   Combine the butter, flour and baking powder, rubbing them together until the mixture is like fine breadcrumbs. Add the yogurt and stir it in well. Gather the pastry together and knead it gently. Refrigerate for an hour or more. Use as required. This recipe makes a nice soft shortcrust pastry, suitable for sweet or savory pies.

Apricot Tart

Serves 4–6

600 ml (1 pt) yogurt
shortcrust pastry to line a tin approximately
    19 cm (7½ in) (see page 147)
400 g (14 oz) canned apricots
90 ml (3 fl oz) whipping cream
2 tbsp cornstarch
50 g (2 oz) superfine sugar
1 tbsp lemon juice
2 tsp vanilla extract
1 egg, separated

1 Drain the yogurt for 3 hours. Bake the pastry case
   for 10 minutes at 180°C/ 350°F/Gas Mark 4. Drain
   the fruit (save the juice for use in a fruit salad)
   and lay the apricot halves on the pastry. When
   the yogurt has drained, mix with the remaining
   ingredients except the egg white, beating
   everything into a smooth mixture.
2 Whisk the egg white until it is stiff and fold it into
   the other mixture. Spoon it over the apricots and
   bake at 170°C/325°F/Gas Mark 3 for 50 minutes.
   (See below).

Variation
Use cottage cheese or quark [225 g (8 oz)] instead of
the yogurt if preferred.

Danish Apple Pie

Serves 4–6

shortcrust pastry to line a tin approximately
    19 cm (7½ in) (see page 147)
5 medium/700 g (1½ lb) cooking
    apples, peeled, cored and sliced
50 ml (2 fl oz) water
50 g (2 oz) sugar
1 tbsp butter
1 tsp ground cinnamon
250 ml (8 fl oz) sour cream
2 tbsp superfine sugar

1 Bake the pastry for 10 minutes at 180°C/350°F/
   Gas Mark 4. Make a thick applesauce using
   the apples, water, sugar, butter and half of the
   cinnamon. There shouldn't be any excess liquid
   when the apples are cooked, but if there is, cook
   for a few minutes more without a lid, stirring to
   prevent the apples from sticking.
2 Let the applesauce cool a little before pouring
   into the pie shell. Spoon the sour cream over the
   apples. Mix the rest of the cinnamon with the
   sugar and sprinkle this over the sour cream. Bake
   at 200°C/400°F/Gas Mark 6 for 30 minutes.
3 This is best served warm, rather than straight from
   the oven, but it is also good cold.

French Apple Tart

Serves 6

75 g (3 oz) unbleached flour
75 g (3 oz) whole wheat flour
50 g (2 oz) ground almonds
8 tbsp butter, softened
1 egg
50 g (2 oz) fruit sugar
pinch salt

Filling

6 cooking apples
10 tbsp butter
2–3 tbsp fruit sugar
2 tsp mixed spice

1 Preheat the oven to 200°C/400°F/Gas Mark 6.
   To make the pastry, sift the flours and almonds
   together onto a board and make a well in the
   middle. Put the remaining ingredients into the well
   and work in with your fingertips until you have a
   smooth dough. Knead for a few minutes, then
   leave for half an hour in the fridge.

2 Meanwhile, peel, core and slice the apples. Heat
   the butter in a saucepan and fry the apples gently
   until soft and golden.

3 Add the sugar and spice and cook, stirring, until
   the apple is coated with syrup.

4 Line a greased 22 cm (8 in) springform pan with
   the pastry and fill with the apple. Bake for 25–30
   minutes and serve with whipped cream.

Continental Cheesecake

Serves 6–8
Sour cream Pastry (see page 148)
6 tbsp butter or margarine
4 tbsp superfine sugar
grated lemon zest
225 g (8 oz) cottage cheese
2 tbsp sour cream
2 eggs, separated
1 tsp vanilla extract

1 Line a 23 cm (9 in) pie plate with the pastry and bake for 5 minutes. Reserve some pastry to decorate the top of the cheesecake. Mix the remaining ingredients except the egg whites together well. Beat the whites until they are stiff and fold them into the mixture.

2 Pour the mixture into the prepared pastry case and bake at 180°C/350°F/Gas Mark 4 for 30 minutes. Decorate with almonds (optional).

Greek Cheesecake

Serves 6
shortcrust pastry to line a tin approximately
    19 cm (7½ in) (see page 147)
450 g (1 lb) cottage cheese
4 eggs
100 g (4 oz) clear honey
1 tsp ground cinnamon

1 Bake the pastry for 15 minutes at 180°C/350°F/Gas Mark 4. Mix the cottage cheese, eggs, honey and cinnamon together well (in a blender or food processor works well). Fill the partially baked pastry case with the mixture and bake it at 180°C/350°F/Gas Mark 4 for 30 minutes.

Pecan Pie

Serves 4–6

250 g (8 oz) Shortcrust Pastry (see page 147)
4 tbsp butter, softened
2 tbsp honey
2 tbsp maple syrup
3 eggs
1 tsp vanilla extract
100 g (4 oz) pecan halves
whipped cream

1   Preheat the oven to 220°C/425°F/Gas Mark 7. Line a 22 cm (8½ in) pan with the pastry. Prick and pre-bake for 10 minutes.
2   Meanwhile, make the filling. Beat the butter together with the honey and syrup until smooth. In another bowl, beat the eggs and vanilla extract thoroughly with a wire or rotary whisk. Pour in the syrup, beating constantly with a fork.
3   Scatter the nuts evenly over the pastry base and pour the custard over. Bake in the middle of the oven for 10 minutes. Reduce the heat to 160°C/325°F/Gas Mark 3 and bake for 25–35 more minutes until the filling is set, but not dry. Serve warm (but not hot) or cold with whipped cream.

Fruit Tartlets

Serves 6–8

100 g (4 oz) cream cheese
½ tsp vanilla extract (optional)
1–2 tsp superfine sugar
6–8 small pastry cases, baked
450 g (1 lb) fresh fruit (raspberries, grapes, strawberries, redcurrants, etc)
apricot jam to glaze

1   Mix the cream cheese with the vanilla and just enough sugar to make a mixture the consistency of thick cream. Spoon into the baked and cooled pie shells. Cover the cream cheese with fresh fruit (de-seed the grapes). Melt a little apricot jam in a saucepan and brush over the fruit to glaze it.
2   Use a selection of different fruits to make an attractive plate of pastries. You could also make one large pie and fill the pie shell with alternate rings of different fruits.

DESSERTS

Fruit fools and trifles, soufflés and mousses, rich ice creams and low-calorie ices are on the menu. There is something for everyone here; from the most sweet-toothed to the carefully diet and health conscious.

Caution Some recipes in this chapter contain raw egg.

Buttermilk Spice Cake

Serves 6
300 g (11 oz) flour
225 g (8 oz) sugar
1½ tsp baking soda
1 tsp baking powder
pinch salt
1 tsp ground cinnamon
½ tsp ground cloves
100 g (4 oz) butter, melted
350 ml (12 fl oz) buttermilk
2 eggs

1 Sift the dry ingredients together. Add the butter and buttermilk and beat the mixture until it is smooth. Pour the batter into a greased and floured cake pan measuring 20 cm (8 in). Bake at 180°C/350°F/Gas Mark 4 for 40 minutes.

Chocolate Cake

Serves 6
100 g (4 oz) butter or soft margarine
175 g (6 oz) sugar
2 eggs, beaten
225 g (8 oz) flour
1 tsp baking powder
4 tbsp/50 g (2 oz) cocoa
1 tsp baking soda
225 ml (8 fl oz) yogurt
1 tsp vanilla extract

1 Beat the butter and sugar together until light and fluffy. Add the eggs and continue beating. Sift the flour, baking powder, cocoa and baking soda, and mix it into the butter mixture. Add the yogurt and vanilla extract, and mix in thoroughly.

2 Pour the mixture into a well greased cake pan, measuring 20 cm (8 in). (Use two sandwich tins or a large ring mold if preferred). Bake at 180°C/350°F/Gas Mark 4 for 25 minutes. Insert a knife to test and cook a little longer if necessary. Timing obviously depends on the type of pan used.

3 Cool and ice, adding 200 g melted chocolate to cream cheese icing (see page 156) or serve sprinkled with icing sugar.

Yogurt Cake

Serves 4

150 ml (5 fl oz) yogurt
250 g (9 oz) flour
3 tsp baking powder
60 ml (2 fl oz) oil
175 g (6 oz) sugar
1 tsp vanilla extract
2 eggs

1 Mix everything together well. Beat until smooth. Pour the mixture into a well-greased cake pan measuring 20 cm (8 in). Bake at 180°C/350°F/Gas Mark 4 for 45 minutes. Insert a knife to test and cook a little longer if necessary.

2 This is a good basic recipe with many variations. To make an upside-down fruit cake, sprinkle the bottom of the pan with brown sugar and lay sliced apples, pears or canned pineapple on the sugar, cover with the cake mixture and cook as directed.

Pumpkin, Sunflower and Raisin Cake

Serves 6–8

350 g (12 oz) pumpkin
225 g (8 oz) whole wheat flour
pinch salt
2 tsp baking powder
1 tsp baking soda
50 g (2 oz) sunflower seeds, chopped
50 g (2 oz) raisins
2 eggs
2 tbsp honey
2 tbsp corn syrup
1 tbsp warm water

1 Preheat the oven to 190°C/375°F/Gas Mark 5. Peel the pumpkin, cut into smallish pieces and boil until tender. Drain and cut up finely.

2 Combine the flour, salt, baking powder, baking soda, sunflower seeds and raisins and mix well.

3 In another bowl, beat the eggs and stir in the honey and corn syrup. Add 1 tbsp of warm water with the pumpkin and beat well.

4 Mix all the ingredients together thoroughly and pour into a greased and floured pan. Bake for 50–60 minutes until done. Allow to stand for 10 minutes in the pan, then cool on a wire rack.

Carrot Cake

Serves 6

6 tbsp butter
250 g (9 oz) superfine sugar
3 eggs
300 g (10 oz) flour
2 tsp baking soda
½ tsp salt
½ tsp ground cinnamon
150 ml (5 fl oz) yogurt
350 g (12 oz) carrots, finely grated
100 g (4 oz) chopped walnuts or mixed nuts

For the icing

2 tbsp unsalted butter
75 g (2½ oz) powdered sugar
grated lemon zest
225 g (8 oz) cream cheese

1 Cream the butter and sugar. Add the eggs one at a time. Sift the flour, baking soda, salt and cinnamon, and add this mixture to the creamed mixture alternately with the yogurt. Fold in the carrots and nuts – mix them in thoroughly but gently.

2 Pour into a greased and floured cake pan measuring 20 cm (8 in). Bake at 180°C/350°F/Gas Mark 4 for 45 minutes. Insert a knife to test and cook a little longer if necessary. Leave to cool on a wire rack.

3 Ice the cake with the Cream Cheese Icing. It is very good on its own if you find the icing too rich.

4 For the icing, mix everything together until smooth – a blender or food processor speeds the work. Refrigerate until firm, then spread on top of the cake. It is also good with the Chocolate Cake (see page 154).

Apple Cake

Serves 6

3 medium cooking apples, peeled, cored
   and sliced
a little cider
1 clove
2 tbsp butter, softened
2 tbsp honey
2 tbsp corn syrup
1 egg
1 tsp mixed spice
pinch salt
2 tsp baking powder
1 tsp baking soda
75 g (3 oz) raisins
175 g (6 oz) whole wheat flour
4 tbsp wheatgerm
1 tsp mixed spice

1   Preheat the oven to 180°C/350°F/Gas Mark 4.
Poach apple slices in a little cider with the clove
until soft. Remove clove. Drain and reserve cider.
Purée apples in a blender.
2   In a large bowl mix butter, honey, corn syrup and 1
tbsp reserved cider. Beat in egg. Stir in apples and
remaining ingredients and mix well.
3   Pour batter into a greased and floured loaf pan,
22 x 10 cm (9 x 4 in), and bake for about an hour
until firm. Allow to stand for 10 minutes, then turn
out of the tin and cool completely on a wire rack.

Fresh Fruit Pudding Cake

Serves 8

2 eggs
75 ml (2½ fl oz) milk
2 tbsp honey
2 tbsp corn syrup
175 g (6 oz) whole wheat flour
1 tsp baking powder
1 tsp baking soda
1 tsp cinnamon
pinch salt
500 g (1 lb) peaches
250 g (½ lb) plums
250 g (½ lb) cherries
100 g (4 oz) walnuts, chopped
a little butter
fresh fruit to decorate
whipped cream

1   Preheat the oven to 200°C/400°F/Gas Mark 6.
Beat the eggs with the milk. Stir in the honey and
corn syrup. Stir in the rest of the dry ingredients
and mix well.
2   Stone and chop the fruit. Mix it into the batter
with the nuts. Pour into a greased and floured
22 cm (9 in) springform pan and bake for 50–60
minutes until set in the middle. Dot with butter
towards the end of the cooking time to prevent the
top drying out.
3   Leave to cool in the pan. Chill in the fridge,
decorate with fresh fruit and serve with
whipped cream.

Crème Caramel

Serves 6
4 tbsp fruit sugar
4 tbsp water

The custard
600 ml (20 fl oz) milk
few drops vanilla extract
4 eggs
3 tbsp fruit sugar

1. Preheat the oven to 350°F/180°C/Gas Mark 4. For the caramel, put the sugar and water in a heavy-based saucepan and stir over a low heat until the sugar has dissolved. Bring to a boil and boil until the syrup is golden. Pour the caramel into six single molds (or one large one) and swirl it around so that it coats the bottom and sides.
2. Bring the milk and vanilla to a boil in a saucepan. Remove from the heat.
3. Beat the eggs and sugar together in a bowl. Gradually add the hot milk, stirring all the while.
4. Strain or ladle the custard into the molds. Stand them in a roasting pan half-filled with hot water and bake for 45 minutes until set. Leave to cool and then chill. Don't turn out the crème caramel until you are ready to serve or it will lose its gloss.

Rhubarb Cream Jello

Serves 6
600 ml (1 pt) yogurt
450 g (1 lb) rhubarb
sugar to taste
1 tsp vanilla extract
½ tsp ground cinnamon or a small piece of cinnamon stick
250 ml (8 fl oz) whipping cream, whipped
2 tbsp agar agar
2 tbsp boiling water

1. Drain the yogurt for about 3 hours.
2. Cook the rhubarb with the sugar, vanilla and cinnamon with just enough water to stop it from burning. You will need 300 ml (10 fl oz) of cooked rhubarb. Mix the cooked rhubarb with the drained yogurt and the whipped cream. Mix gently until everything is combined.
3. Dissolve the agar agar in the boiling water, mixing well until smooth. Add to the rhubarb mixture, stirring the agar agar in quickly. Turn the mixture into a moistened small ring mold and chill until set. Serve with more whipped cream if desired.

Variation
Use 225 g (8 oz) quark, cream cheese or cottage cheese if preferred instead of the drained yogurt.

Blackcurrant Snow

Serves 4
150 ml (5 fl oz) yogurt
2 eggs, separated
1 tbsp crème de cassis (or blackcurrant syrup)
50 g (2 oz) superfine sugar
225 g (8 oz) blackcurrants

1 Stir the yogurt and egg yolks together with the crème de cassis and sugar until the sugar is dissolved.
2 Just before serving, whisk the egg whites until stiff and fold them into the yolk mixture. Fold the blackcurrants in gently. Spoon into single dishes.
3 Serve with sponge fingers or cookies.

Variation

Change the flavors by using a different liqueur: orange liqueur with a little grated orange zest, or chocolate liqueur with some grated chocolate. If you want to prepare this some time before serving it, refrigerate the yolk mixture and add the whites and blackcurrants at the last minute.

Orange Chiffon

Serves 4–6
1 tbsp agar agar
100 ml (4 fl oz) orange juice
5 tbsp superfine sugar
2 eggs, separated
250 ml (8 fl oz) buttermilk
grated orange zest

1 Soak the agar agar in orange juice. Heat gently until the agar agar is dissolved. Remove the saucepan from the heat. Beat 3 tbsp sugar with the egg yolks until light and fluffy. Add this to the agar agar mixture and stir it over very low heat until it begins to thicken. Pour the thickened mixture into a bowl and add the buttermilk and orange peel. Mix together and chill until it is beginning to set.
2 Beat the egg whites until they are stiff. Fold in the remaining sugar. Combine the egg whites and the agar agar mixture, stirring gently.
3 Pour the chiffon into a serving dish (or use single glasses) and refrigerate until needed.

Orange Cream

Serves 4
2 eggs, separated
2 tbsp superfine sugar
juice and grated zest of 1 orange
225 g (8 oz) cream cheese
2 tbsp orange flavored liqueur

1　Beat the egg yolks with the sugar until thick and creamy. Add the orange juice and zest and mix it in well. Soften the cheese and add it to the egg mixture. Add the liqueur.

2　Beat the whites until they are stiff. Fold a little of the beaten whites into the cheese mixture and then gently fold in the rest. Spoon into four glasses and serve immediately.

3　If you want to prepare this in advance, leave the egg whites until just before you are going to serve, and whisk the whites and fold them into the cheese mixture at the very last minute. If you make it in advance with the egg whites it may separate – if this happens, stir through before serving.

Damson Mousse

Serves 4
450 g (1 lb) damsons or other plums
sugar to taste
250 ml (8 fl oz) water
1 tbsp agar agar
3 tbsp boiling water
150 ml (¼ pt) yogurt
2 egg whites

1　Cook the damsons with sugar and water. Rub the cooked fruit through a sieve to make a thick purée. Check the sweetness and add further sugar if necessary.

2　Dissolve the agar agar in the boiling water and add it to the purée. Leave the mixture to cool, and when it is beginning to set, fold in the yogurt. Beat the egg whites until they are stiff. Add a little of the beaten whites to the damson mixture to lighten it and then fold in the rest of the whites.

3　Refrigerate for a minimum of 6 hours – overnight if possible. The longer you leave it, the better the flavor.

Variation
Try this well-flavored plums or other stewed fruit.

Russian Pashka

Serves 6

175 g (6 oz) superfine sugar
175 g (6 oz) unsalted butter
2 egg yolks
350 g (12 oz) cottage cheese, drained
   and sieved
150 ml (¼ pt) sour cream or whipping cream
225 g (8 oz) mixed dried fruit
1 tsp vanilla extract

1 Cream the sugar and butter together until it is light and fluffy. Beat in the egg yolks one at a time. Add the cottage cheese to the butter mixture and mix well together. Add the remaining ingredients, mixing them all in well.

2 Pour the mixture into a serving dish and refrigerate for a minimum of 2 hours.

Chestnut Whips

Serves 4

425 g (15 oz) can unsweetened chestnut purée
2 tbsp dark rum
1 tbsp dark brown sugar
150 ml (5 fl oz) strained Greek yogurt
2 egg whites
chopped chestnuts or pistachios

1 Beat the chestnut purée, rum, sugar and yogurt together until smooth.

2 Whisk the egg whites until stiff and fold into the chestnut mixture.

3 Spoon into one large or four single serving dishes. Chill for 1 hour, decorate with chopped nuts and serve.

Cheese Blintzes

Makes 8–9 pancakes

Crepes recipe ingredients (see page 61)
350 g (12 oz) cottage cheese
1 egg yolk
1 tbsp sugar
butter

1 Make the crepes. Mix the cheese, egg yolk and sugar together well. Put a spoonful of the mixture onto the cooked side of each crepe and make a square parcel by folding two edges into the middle and then folding the remaining two edges over.

2 Melt a little butter and fry the filled crepes, folded side down first, turning over to fry the second side until lightly browned. Serve hot.

Rose Petal Trifle

Serves 6
2 eggs
4 tbsp/dark brown sugar
½ tsp ground cinnamon
4 tbsp whole wheat flour
4 tbsp all-purpose flour
1 tbsp polyunsaturated margarine, melted
2 egg yolks
2 tbsp cornstarch
2 tbsp light brown sugar
300 ml (½ pt) skim milk
1 tbsp triple-strength rosewater
4 passion fruits, halved
175 g (6 oz) raspberries
2 tbsp whipping cream or strained
   Greek yogurt
edible rose petals

1 Line and lightly grease an 18 cm (7 in) cake pan. Whisk the eggs and dark brown sugar together, until thick and creamy.
2 Fold in the cinnamon, flours and melted margarine. Pour into the pan and bake in a preheated oven at 350°F/180°C/Gas Mark 4 for 20 minutes, or until risen and firm. Turn out and cool.
3 Beat the egg yolks, cornstarch and light brown sugar together. Heat the milk until boiling and pour onto the egg mix. Return to the saucepan and cook, stirring continuously, over a gentle heat until thickened.
4 Add the rosewater, cover and set aside until cold.
5 Cut the cake into cubes and place in the base of a serving dish. Scoop the flesh from the passion fruit and spoon over the cake. Top with raspberries.
6 Pour over the custard and pipe the cream, or spoon the yogurt on top. Garnish with rose petals and serve.

Raspberry and Apple Layer

Serves 6
450 g (1 lb) pudding apples, peeled, cored and chopped
225 g (8 oz) ripe raspberries, puréed
1 tbsp light brown sugar
2 tbsp polyunsaturated margarine
50 g (2 oz) whole wheat breadcrumbs
100 g (4 oz) Muesli Cookies (see page 146), crushed
1 tsp mixed spice
raspberries
green apple slices

1 Place the apples in a saucepan with 1 tbsp water, cover and gently cook until tender. Beat or process in a blender or food processor into a purée.
2 Mix with the raspberry purée and sugar. Leave to cool.
3 Melt the margarine in a saucepan, add the breadcrumbs and stir over low heat until browned. Stir in the Muesli Cookies and mixed spice. Place the fruit purée and crumb mix in alternate layers in glass bowls. Decorate with fruit and serve.

Banana and Cherry Yogurt

Serves 4
4 very ripe bananas, cut into pieces
2 tsp lemon juice
300 ml (10 fl oz) natural low-fat yogurt
225 g (8 oz) fresh cherries, stoned
cherry pairs with stalks

1 Mash the bananas with the lemon juice. Mix in the yogurt.
2 Divide the stoned cherries between four tall glasses and top with the banana yogurt.
3 Hang a pair of cherries over the edge of each glass to decorate. You can serve it chilled, alone or with wholewheat biscuits.

Berry Meringue

Serves 4–6
crushed meringues to line a 18 cm (7 in)
   baking dish
350 g (12 oz) blackberries
150 ml (¼ pt) sour cream
2 tsp superfine sugar
½ tsp vanilla extract

1 Line the baking dish with the crushed meringues. Cover with the blackberries. Mix the sour cream, sugar and vanilla extract together and spoon this over the berries. Bake at 350°F/180°C/Gas Mark 4 for 20 minutes.

Cook's Tip
If you make a lot of meringues you may well suffer from a surfeit of crushed meringues – here is the answer to the problem. Other berries would do but blackberries have a particular acidity that contrasts with the sweetness of the meringues.

Buckwheat Crepes with Blueberries

Makes 9 small crepes
40 g (1½ oz) whole wheat flour
pinch salt
1 egg
150 ml (5 fl oz) milk
1 tbsp melted butter

To serve
500 g (1 lb) blueberries
4 tbsp honey
fresh strawberries to serve

1 To make the crepes mixture, sift the flour and salt into a bowl. Make a well in the middle of it and add the egg.

2 Gradually beat in the milk. When half of the milk has been added, beat in the melted butter. Continue beating in the milk until you have a thin batter. Allow the batter to stand for half an hour.

3 Meanwhile, prepare the filling. Wash and pick over the blueberries. Put them in a heavy-bottomed saucepan over a very low flame. It is best to add no water at all. When the fruit is submerged in its own juice, add the honey and stir until dissolved. The syrup should be thick and fruity.

4 To make the crepes, oil a heavy-bottomed saucepan 18 cm (7 in) in diameter. Place it on the flame and, when it is very hot, add 2 tbsp/of the batter. Tilt the saucepan so that the batter covers the base. Cook until the crepe is beginning to brown on the underside and then turn over and cook the other side. You may have to throw the first crepe away, as it will absorb the excess oil in the saucepan.

5 Continue making crepes, keeping them warm, until all the batter has been used up.

6 Serve the crepes with honey, blueberries and strawberries to garnish.

Toffee Bananas

Serves 4

4 bananas, peeled
1 egg
2 tbsp all-purpose flour
oil for deep frying
4 tbsp sugar
1 tbsp cold water

1 Cut the bananas in half lengthways and then cut each half in two crossways.
2 Beat the egg, add the flour and mix well to make a smooth batter.
3 Heat the oil in a wok or deep fryer. Coat each piece of banana with batter and deep fry until golden. Remove and drain.
4 Pour off the excess oil, leaving about 1 tbsp oil in the wok or deep fryer. Add the sugar and water and stir over medium heat to dissolve the sugar. Continue stirring and, when the sugar has caramelized, add the hot banana pieces. Coat well and remove. Dip the hot bananas in cold water to harden the toffee and serve immediately.

Apple Yogurt Dessert

Serves 4–6

600 ml (1 pt) yogurt
150 ml (5 fl oz) whipping cream
2 eggs
4 tbsp superfine sugar
grated lemon zest
1 large cooking apple, peeled and sliced
½ tsp ground cinnamon
2 tbsp sugar

1 Drain the yogurt for about 4 hours. Whip the cream and fold it into the drained yogurt. Beat the eggs with the sugar and lemon zest and add to the yogurt mixture.
2 Pour into a greased shallow oven dish. Lay the apple slices on top of the yogurt mixture. Scatter cinnamon on top and then the sugar.
3 Bake at 180°C/350°F/Gas mark 4 for 50 minutes. Serve warm.

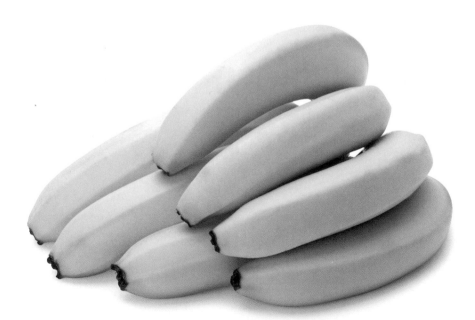

Apple, Strawberry and Blackberry Crumble

Serves 4
4 cooking apples
1 tbsp honey
100 g (4 oz) strawberries
100 g (4 oz) blackberries
225 g (8 oz) whole wheat flour
100 g (4 oz) butter
2 tbsp sesame seeds
1 tsp mixed spice
pinch salt

1 Preheat the oven to 180°C/350°F/Gas mark 4. Peel and core the apples and cut into slices. Put apples in a shallow ovenproof dish with a little water and the honey and cook, covered, in the oven for 30 minutes.
2 Meanwhile, hull and slice the strawberries and pick over the blackberries.
3 Now make the crumble. Place the remaining ingredients in a bowl and rub in the butter with your fingers until the mixture resembles fine breadcrumbs.
4 When the apples are ready, mix in the strawberries and blackberries, adding a little more honey if desired. Press the crumble mixture gently on top of the fruit and return to the oven for 15 minutes until golden brown. Serve hot or cold with cream.

Baked Apples

Serves 4
4 cooking apples, cored
2 tbsp butter
2 tbsp sugar
150 ml (¼ pt) yogurt
2 tbsp brown sugar
75 g (2½ oz) chopped nuts

1 Score the apples around the middle. Place them in a shallow baking dish. Mix the butter and sugar together and fill the center of each apple with the mixture.
2 Bake the apples uncovered at 200°C/400°F/Gas mark 6 for 20 minutes. Mix the yogurt with the brown sugar and nuts and pour this mixture over the baked apples. Return to the oven for 10 more minutes. Serve hot.

Clementine Cups

Serves 4
4 clementines
juice 1 orange
¾ sachet powdered agar agar
1 tsp clear honey
6 tbsp strained Greek yogurt
1 egg white
1 clementine, peel and pith removed, segmented
evergreen leaves
grated plain carob bar

1 Remove the tops from the clementines. Carefully scoop out all the flesh and reserve the shells.
2 Press the fruit through a sieve to extract the juice
3 Mix with the orange juice. Sprinkle the agar agar over 3 tbsp juice in a small saucepan and heat gently to dissolve. Stir in the honey and place in the bowl. Add the remaining juice and leave until almost set. Fold in the yogurt. Whip the egg white until stiff and fold in.
4 Refrigerate until the mixture holds its shape, place in shells and chill until set. Serve with clementine segments and grated carob.

Lemon Soufflé

Serves 4–6
3 eggs, separated
175 g (6 oz) superfine sugar
6 tbsp flour
4 tbsp lemon juice
lemon zest, grated
350 ml (12 fl oz) yogurt
powdered sugar

1   Mix the egg yolks with all the remaining ingredients in a heatproof bowl. Place the bowl over a saucepan of simmering water and cook until you have a mixture the consistency of thick cream, stirring constantly. Remove the bowl from the heat.
2   Beat the egg whites until stiff. Fold them into the cooled mixture.
3   Pour it into a buttered soufflé dish, measuring 18 x 7½ cm (7 x 3 in), or into individual ramekins or oven-proof cups, and cook at 170°C/325°F/Gas Mark 3 for 40 minutes. Sprinkle with powdered sugar before serving.

Pear Soufflé

Serves 4–6

450 g (1 lb) pears
1–2 tbsp butter
a little honey
pinch cinnamon
3 large eggs, separated

1. Preheat the oven to 200°C/400°F/Gas Mark 6.
2. Peel, halve and core the pears. Cut them into slices.
3. Heat the butter in a saucepan and add the pear slices. When the fruit has softened, raise the heat a little, break up the fruit with a wooden spoon and cook until mushy.
4. Put the contents of the saucepan into a blender. Blend until smooth and add a little honey and cinnamon to taste. Pour into a bowl and beat in the egg yolks.
5. Butter a 1.8 litre (4 pts) soufflé dish. Whisk the egg whites until they form soft peaks and fold into the mixture. Pour into the soufflé dish and bake in the oven for 20–25 minutes until just golden brown and nearly set.

Vanilla Soufflé

Serves 4–6

600 ml (1 pt) yogurt
6 tbsp butter, softened
3 eggs, separated
1 tsp vanilla extract
150 g (5 oz) superfine sugar

1. Drain the yogurt for about 4 hours. Mix the drained yogurt with the butter, egg yolks and vanilla extract. Beat the egg whites until they are stiff and fold in the sugar. Fold a little of the egg white mixture into the yogurt mixture to lighten it and then carefully fold in the rest.
2. Butter and lightly flour a small soufflé dish, measuring 18 x 7½ cm (7 x 3 in). Pour the mixture into the dish and bake at 190°C/375°F/Gas Mark 5 for 30 minutes.

Fruity Yogurt Cassata

Serves 4

225 g (8 oz) soft dried apricots
300 ml (½ pt) grapefruit juice
2 egg whites
225 g (8 oz) strained Greek yogurt
50 g (2 oz) golden raisins
25 g (1 oz) flaked almonds
mint sprigs

1. Place the apricots and grapefruit juice in a saucepan, bring to a boil, cover and simmer for 10 minutes, until apricots are soft. Purée in a food processor and leave to cool and thicken.
2. Fold the yogurt into the apricot purée and place in a freezerproof container. Freeze for 1½–2 hours, or until the edges become softly frozen.
3. Whisk the egg whites until stiff. Mix the yogurt ice together and fold in the golden raisins, almonds and egg whites. Return to the freezer for 3–4 hours. until frozen. Garnish with sprigs of mint.

Carob Upside-down Pudding

Serves 4
2 small pears, peeled, cored and halved
2 eggs, separated
3 tbsp/40 g (1½ oz) dark brown sugar
1½ tbsp carob powder
2 tbsp plain whole wheat flour
2 tbsp ground almonds
1 tbsp clear honey
kumquat slices

1 Arrange the pears in the base of an 18 cm (7 in) round cake pan, which has been lightly greased.
2 Whisk the egg yolks with the sugar until light and creamy. Whisk in 1 tbsp hot water and the carob powder. Fold in the flour and almonds.
3 Whisk the egg whites until stiff and fold into the carob mix. Pour over the pears and cook in a preheated oven at 190°C/375°F/Gas mark 5 for 35 minutes.

Carrot Halva

Serves 4–6
450 g (1 lb) carrots, peeled and grated
900 ml (2 pt) milk
150 g (5 oz) sugar
3 green cardamom pods
4 tbsp) Ghee (see page 115)
2 tbsp raisins
2 tbsp pistachio nuts, skinned and chopped

1 Place the carrots, milk, sugar and cardamoms in a large saucepan and bring to a boil. Lower heat to medium low and, stirring occasionally, cook until all the liquid has evaporated.
2 Heat the ghee in a large frying pan over medium heat, add the cooked carrots, raisins and pistachios and, stirring constantly, fry for 15–20 minutes until it is dry and is reddish in color. Serve hot or cold.

Yogurt with Saffron

Serves 4

600 ml (1 pt) yogurt

¼ tsp saffron

1 tbsp warm milk

100 g (4 oz) superfine sugar

2 tbsp pistachio nuts, skinned and chopped

1 Put the yogurt in a muslin bag and hang it up for 4–5 hours to get rid of the excess water.
2 Soak the saffron in the milk for 30 minutes.
3 Whisk together the drained yogurt, sugar and saffron milk until smooth and creamy.
4 Put in a dish and garnish with the nuts. Chill until set.

Couers à La Crème

Serves 4

250 g (8 oz) cream cheese

100 g (4 oz) yogurt

250 g (8 oz) strawberries

150 ml (¼ pt) half and half

1–2 tbsp honey

1 Blend the cream cheese with the yogurt and pack into the small heart-shaped molds traditional for this dessert. Chill.
2 Make a strawberry sauce by blending half the strawberries with the cream and honey. Unmold the cheeses onto single plates, surround with the sauce and decorate with the remaining strawberries.

Orange Buttermilk Ice

Serves 4

2 eggs

50 g (2 oz) superfine sugar

175 ml (6 fl oz) corn syrup

450 ml (16 fl oz) buttermilk

150 ml (¼ pt) orange juice

grated zest of orange

1 Blend everything together well. Freeze for a minimum of 3 hours. Blend again until smooth and return to the freezer. Freeze overnight or longer. (This ice stays remarkably soft even when frozen for some weeks).

Acknowledgements

The publishers would like to thank the following picture libraries for their kind permission to use their pictures:

Istock: 26,34, 36, 47, 63, 67, 72, 147, 154, 167,

Shutterstock: 7, 8, 12, 14, 16, 17, 19, 20, 21, 24, 27, 28, 31, 32, 33, 35, 37, 39, 41, 42, 43, 45, 46, 48, 51, 54, 55, 57, 58, 59, 61, 69, 71, 73, 74, 76, 78, 80, 81, 83, 84, 86, 92, 95, 100, 103, 104, 109, 111, 112, 114, 116, 122, 125, 129, 133, 140, 141, 144, 145, 150, 152, 153 155, 156, 158, 160, 163, 164, 165,

Photocuisine: 88, 90

Stockfood: front cover, 65, 82, 106, 117, 126, 146, 169, 171

Every effort has been made to contact the copyright holders for images reproduced in this book. The Publisher would welcome any errors or omissions being brought to their attention and apologizes in advance for any unintentional omissions or errors. The Publisher will be pleased to insert the appropriate acknowledgement to any companies or individuals in any subsequent edition of the work.